St. George Jackson Mivart

Contemporary Evolution

An Essay on Some Recent Social Changes

St. George Jackson Mivart

Contemporary Evolution

An Essay on Some Recent Social Changes

ISBN/EAN: 9783743382572

Manufactured in Europe, USA, Canada, Australia, Japa

Cover: Foto ©Thomas Meinert / pixelio.de

Manufactured and distributed by brebook publishing software (www.brebook.com)

St. George Jackson Mivart

Contemporary Evolution

Contemporary Evolution.

AN ESSAY

ON SOME RECENT SOCIAL CHANGES.

BY

ST. GEORGE MIVART.

NEW YORK:
D. APPLETON AND COMPANY,
549 AND 551 BROADWAY.
1876.

TO THE MOST HONOURABLE
THE MARQUIS OF RIPON, K.G.

My dear Lord Ripon,

I am very sensible of the kindness which has so readily accorded me permission to dedicate to your Lordship this Essay on Contemporary Evolution.

I might indeed feel diffidence in thus attempting to point out some unlooked-for results of those post-mediæval social changes, in effecting which the English-speaking races have borne so prominent a part, but for this encouraging permission from one whose enlarged and candid mind renders him a most competent however indulgent a judge of my endeavour.

With much respect,

I am,

My dear Lord Ripon,

Yours most sincerely,

St. GEORGE MIVART.

March 25th, 1876.
Wilmshurst, Uckfield.

CONTENTS.

CHAPTER I.
INTRODUCTORY . . . 1

CHAPTER II.
POLITICAL EVOLUTION . . . 45

CHAPTER III.
THREE IDEALS 79

CHAPTER IV.
SCIENTIFIC EVOLUTION 131

CHAPTER V.
PHILOSOPHIC EVOLUTION 164

CHAPTER VI.
ÆSTHETIC EVOLUTION 218

Contemporary Evolution.

CHAPTER I.

INTRODUCTORY.

THE inexperienced traveller who, having been wearied by the repeated slow ascents and drag-wheeled descents of a tedious coach road, afterwards surveys from a neighbouring mountain the route he has pursued, may not improbably feel surprise at the inconspicuousness of undulations which, while being traversed, seemed so considerable.

The survey of the path of human social evolution from a stand-point as yet inaccessible to us, would no doubt in most cases similarly affect that estimate of the importance of his own epoch which each observer, reflecting on contemporary social phenomena, is apt to form.

Nevertheless, as in spite of the relative evenness of the world's surface as a whole, there *are* here and there exceptional conditions — sheer precipices of both ascent and descent; so history exhibits parallel phenomena which exceptionally demarcate comparatively uneventful areas.

Amidst the grassy plains of North-western America,

one region has obtained the title of "*Mauvaise Terre*," from the numerous furrows and depressions by which progression is again and again arrested. Farther south, the great Rio Colorado has by the secular attrition of its stream worn for itself a course here and there bounded by parallel precipices descending vertically some five hundred feet or more from the level plain above, and forming the celebrated cañons of California.

The slow, secular action of social change has resulted here and there, under special conditions, in the production of more or less sudden and abrupt manifestations, serving for all future time as sociological landmarks, cañons on the plain of history.

If a Greek who had watched the solemn procession of the crocus-coloured Peplos to the Parthenon on the great Panathenaic festival, or had laughed with Aristophanes at the tiresome old sophist whose moral obstetrics wearied his ears as his ugliness offended his Attic taste for beauty; or if one of the succeeding generation who, having listened in the Pnyx to a philippic from the greatest orator who ever filled the *bema*, consoled himself for existing political troubles with Herodotus or with Homer,—if either of these Greeks, reflecting on his surroundings, deemed himself a witness of a social culmination in art, the drama, oratory, history, and poetry, constituting his fellow-citizens the models and the teachers of mankind for thousands of years to come, he would *not* have been in error, would not have over-estimated the significance of his epoch.

A Roman who had just witnessed the decapitation of a criminal for violating the laws and defying the majesty of the state by refusing to burn incense to the gods and to invoke the genius of the emperor, might have reflected that the criminal was one of a class possessed by an "*exitiabilis superstitio*" and a certain "*odium humani generis*," who met together at night amidst the dead to sing "charms" and adore with magic rites a crucified malefactor represented with an ass's head, and who were so rapidly and mysteriously increasing that no citizen could feel quite sure he might not even himself be seized unwittingly by this degrading and insane superstition, — had such a Roman, so reflecting, considered his era to be one critical for the empire, and himself a witness of the commencement of a social cataclysm, he would *not* have exaggerated the importance of the phenomena surrounding him.

A refined Florentine, revelling in the brilliancy of a reviving Platonism (which was beginning to replace what he deemed "narrow scholasticism," as the noble classical architecture was banishing the endlessly repeated details of the latest Gothic), and hospitably entertaining a Spanish Jew whom mendacious conformity had failed to screen from the jealous scrutiny of the Inquisition of 1495, and who in turn regaled his host with strange details of the plants, animals, and men brought from the lately discovered western lands to Castile,—such a Florentine, if he (considering the coincidence of the disinterment of an old world with the discovery of a new) consoled his Israelitish guest with the assurance that they were the beholders of events destined to result in the overthrow of the existing theocratic forms, would in no way have overstated the consequence and meaning of the period in which he lived.

That spectator who in 1789—when witnessing the long train of black-coated members of the "*tiers état*" preceding the plumed nobles and brilliant court on their way to the solemn mass of the Holy Ghost before the opening of the States-General—exclaimed, "There goes the funeral procession of the French monarchy," showed a remarkably correct appreciation of the fatal significance of the passing pageant. Not, of course, but that the conditions for the coming explosion had been slowly, almost imperceptibly, accumulating for centuries before; yet the fact of such accumulation in no way detracts from the truth that the end of the eighteenth century in France will be for ever memorable as the epoch of the actual occurrence of those changes which had taken so long in becoming proximately potential.

We in England (and, indeed, in Europe generally) may not improbably be traversing an epoch destined to be memorable for a long time to come, and one which many deem to be as critical as, even if not more so than, either of the two periods last referred to; and this for two reasons.

First, because it may prove to be the occasion for the open and complete manifestation of latent tendencies which those two periods but imperfectly revealed.

Secondly, because present changes are distinguished from all that have gone before by their intense self-consciousness. As was well remarked by Mr. Tylor in the *Contemporary Review**: "Our social science has a new character and power, inasmuch as we live near a turning-point in the history of mankind. The *unconscious* evolution of society is giving place to its *conscious* development."

To perceive that we are living in a critical epoch is one thing, to appraise that epoch and estimate its tendencies correctly is another and a much more difficult one. No one of course can withdraw himself completely from the special influence of his age and country, however vigorous may be his will or extensive his culture; yet to estimate such phenomena correctly, and with as little bias as possible, is about the most important task to which a thinker can in these days apply his intellect.

It is so supremely important, because we are all called upon to contribute to social evolution, and more or less distinctly to take sides, and of course only by rare ac-

---

* For June, 1873, p. 72.

cident can beneficial action directly result from erroneous judgments.

How easily erroneous sociological judgments may be formed by the most able and generally best informed men recent events make singularly plain to us.

Those who are old enough to recollect the passing of the first Reform Bill, and have sympathetically followed the train of political ideas thenceforward popular, can hardly fail to view with amazement the more recent acts or manifestoes of advocates of Liberalism. Our comic journals were never tired of ridiculing everything military; free-trade and toleration were ideals, and in 1851 idyllic rhapsodies celebrated the speedy end of wars and the apotheoses of Watt and Arkwright.

As to religious liberty, except that feeble persecution might linger in the benighted peninsulas of South-western Europe, it was treason to doubt its maintenance and triumphant propagation. Lord Brougham—the eloquent representative of the whole school—spoke of the "evil spirits of tyranny and persecution which haunted the long night now *gone down the sky*," while there were few of his sympathisers but would have scouted the idea that theological conceptions could again have force to involve Europe in bloody struggles, or that the advocates of any form of Christianity would be almost tempted to defend themselves sword in hand against the oppression of their persecutors.

This falsification of such benevolent hopes, as also of the pontifical vaticinations of Auguste Comte, is a demonstration that the current Liberal conception of social philosophy as applied to recent and contemporaneous phenomena was inadequate, just as the philosophy accepted at the period of the great French Revolution was proved by the event to have been superficial and delusory, and as the ideas which found expression in that most fascinating period the early *Renaissance*, gave no warning of dire events to come like the Thirty Years' War and the bloody and prolonged struggle of the League.

Social and political events being as they are the ultimate outcome of the involved interaction of most numerous, complex, and remote causes, it is evident that such causes must be sought in conditions antedating by many centuries the events we would seek to explain. This truth has been perceived and acted on by all who of late have occupied themselves with the Philosophy of History, and have, like De Tocqueville, sought to trace out such hidden connections. No writer would any longer venture to explain the crisis of 1789 exclusively by the reigns of the fifteenth and sixteenth Louis, or that of 1688 only by the corruption and errors of the Restoration.

The great prominence which religious questions have of late assumed is, as has just been remarked, strangely in contrast with the expectations generally prevalent before the outbreak of 1848. Now our daily press seeks again and again to impress on its readers that the fundamental questions and divisions amongst men are religious ones, while every sort of journal remarks on, deplores, or exults in, the widespread process of religious disintegration, and predicts or speculates about possible reconstructions.

The very same character of religious excitation marks, however, both the French revolutionary epoch and the period of the Renaissance as well as that in which we now live; nor would it be denied by many of our more philosophical thinkers, that the most striking phenomena of these three periods are but indications of different stages of one prolonged movement, though such thinkers would differ as to the nature and tendency of the movement itself.

Three questions then seem to demand our attention.

I. The first of these is, Whether in fact one spirit and tendency has or has not really animated these great movements which have marked the post-mediæval epoch?

II. The second question is, If there has been one such inspiration, what has been its true nature and character?

III. The third question is, What is likely to be the further effect of such a spirit, and is it likely henceforward to increase or to diminish?

Complex and difficult as the first question may appear

at the outset, it does not seem difficult to fix upon a leading characteristic whereby to connect together, on the one hand, the period of the Renaissance with that of the Revolution; on the other, the latter event with contemporaneous phenomena.

That wide-spread break-up of definite religious systems, accompanied by a more or less marked tendency to democracy in politics, which exists to-day, is generally allowed to be the expression of a spirit similar to, if not identical with, that which predominantly influenced the great French movement of the last century.

Similarly, the affected imitation of ancient Rome, the studious reproduction of classical customs, which were practised by so many of the "citizens" of France, as well as by its "senators" and "consuls," marks a certain similarity of spirit between the revolutionary movement of the eighteenth century and the elegant and refined period of the Renaissance.

Moreover, though the last-named period was not, except more or less in Italy, avowedly anti-Christian (like the French Revolution), it was, nevertheless, speedily followed by religious disruptions, which are deemed by many who heartily approve them as but the logical precursors of that absolute negation of Christianity which has, in fact, become so widespread in Switzerland, Germany, France, and Holland, and is now openly avowed by many of those who lineally represent the initiators of such disruptions.

One spirit then may, at least to a certain extent, be said to have influenced the course of events from the commencing disintegration of mediæval civilisation down to the present day. Such, at least appears at first sight, to be the case. Further reflection may, or may not, confirm this view, and may indicate what is the true nature of that spirit.

The persistence of national characteristics, and the strange latent vitality of apparently extinct modes of thought and feeling, frequently cause surprise.

In how many respects do not the Gauls of Cæsar live to-day under the presidency of the gallant marshal, Duke of Magenta?

Who can fail to see in Prince Bismarck the representative of one of those Teutons who gained baptism through the sword of Charlemagne, and who in turn now seeks, consciously or unconsciously, to replace the symbol of the Cross by the hammer of Thor, and the last relics of a Christian polity by an avowed system of "blood and iron."

In the existing Spanish civil war between the Carlist north and the passionately democratic south with its strong infusion of Moorish blood, we see (whatever may be its result) a certain resemblance to that struggle between the Mahometan hosts and those Christians who in the fortresses of the Pyrenees turned the tide of the Saracenic invasion.

In Belgium, the conflict of the sixteenth century in a

modified form still endures, and the very name of "Gueux" is now assumed by those who represent the spirit of the original bearers of that appellation.

We all recollect Gibbon's vivid picture of the complete restoration by Artaxerxes of the old religion of Persia, which had lingered on in spite of an apparent interruption dating back from the Alexandrian conquest—a noteworthy instance of persistence in ancient times.

To-day, French missionaries find to their amazement that in spite of a persecution deemed exterminating, Christianity in Japan still flourishes, having been secretly handed down for generations without the aid of a single priest, and with no sacraments but baptism and matrimony.

If survival and revival may ensue under such circumstances, surely a system of unknown antiquity, universal in extent and eminently congenial to most men as they actually exist, may be confidently expected to possess a life of extreme tenacity and to show an increasing tendency to revival as impediments and restrictions are successively removed.

Such a system was that essentially pantheistic paganism and nature-worship which Christianity seemed for a time, in Europe, to have so thoroughly succeeded in supplanting.

Even, however, at that period which has by common consent been accepted as representing the culmination of the mediæval theocracy and of the purely Christian monarchy—the epoch, that is, of Innocent III. and of St. Louis—the spirit of paganism was far enough from being extinct, as is evidenced to us by a multitude of local superstitions, by such institutions as the *fête des fous*, and by the wide-spread belief in, and practice of, magic rites. Nay, already it showed signs of returning strength and activity in the poetry of Provence, the legend of Héloise and Abelard, and various kindred phenomena, constituting what has been well termed* the "Mediæval Renaissance."

To this very day, according to some writers, the Baal fires of Phœnicia live in the Norwegian bonfires of St. John's Eve.

The talismans against the evil eye, so common in Naples, are almost as expressive of paganism as the forbidden emblems, sold as late as 1790† in the neighbourhood of the rocky mound with its old round church dedicated to SS. Cosmo e Damiano.

"Even recently an oak copse at Loch Siant, in the Isle of Skye, was held so sacred that no person would venture to cut the smallest branch from it." The pilgrims at St. Fillan's well in 1791, "walked or were carried deasil (*sunwise*) round the well. They also threw each a white

---

* By Walter H. Pater, Fellow of Brasenose College, Oxford, in his "Studies in the History of the Renaissance."

† To Sir Richard Colt Hoare.

stone on an adjacent cairn, and left behind a scrap of their clothing as an offering."*

"The Carinthian peasant will fodder the wind by setting a dish of food in a tree before his house, and the fire by casting in lard and dripping, in order that gale and conflagration may not hurt him. At least up to the end of the last century, this most direct elemental sacrifice might be seen in Germany at the midsummer festival in the most perfect form; some of the porridge from the table was thrown into the fire, and some into running water, some was buried in the earth, and some smeared on leaves and put on the chimney-top for the winds." In France, at Andrieux in Dauphiny, "at the solstice the villagers went out upon the bridge when the sun rose, and offered him an omelet. The custom of burning alive the finest calf to save a murrain-struck herd had its examples in Cornwall in the present century."†

At the vintage festival of the Madonna del Arco, signs of practices connected with the old Greek nature-worship reappear in the leaf-wreathed poles brandished by youths, themselves garnished with strings of filberts on their necks and arms—their juice-smeared faces shaded by wreaths of vine-leaves.

It is not, however, to such mere external practices that

---

* Quoted by Sir John Lubbock in his "Origin of Civilisation," pp. 192 and 198.
† See Edward B. Tylor's "Primitive Culture," vol. ii. pp. 369, 370.

it is here intended mainly to direct attention, but to a deeper underlying spirit. Such phenomena are patent survivals likely to long linger amidst an unlettered peasantry, the sons of the Pagani of earlier Christian times. The movements of the sixteenth and eighteenth centuries sprang rather from above than below, and the anti-Christian developments of to-day are mainly due to men of culture and education not generally intent upon a restoration of paganism, nor consciously imbued with its spirit.

Nevertheless, it is here maintained that the deeply pantheistic and pagan spirit with which the Aryan mind was once saturated (which shows itself superficially in the modern practices just referred to) profoundly modifies and actuates, not the minds of the poor only, but of the rich and educated, who, from whatever cause, have either failed to master or who (in rare instances) having mastered have deliberately rejected Christian philosophy and theology. The result is the assumption of no merely negative attitude towards Christianity, but of a profound and violent antagonism to it springing from a keen, often passionate, attachment to an opposed system.

It is happily very possible to attribute this antagonism in the case of many to a narrow zeal for truth partially apprehended. The beauty, the truth, and the goodness of nature when revealed to some men with a force and vivacity new and strange seem to them to be incompatible with the supernaturalism of Christianity.

The extreme narrowness and want of flexibility of many minds are nothing less than amazing, and the effects of "bias" have been lately well illustrated by Mr. Herbert Spencer.*

It is then little to be wondered at that when, after centuries of comparative neglect, the study of nature was resumed with energy and passion, an accompanying depreciation of the Christian supernatural should have manifested itself, and the wonder becomes even less when it is recollected how such revived naturalistic tendencies harmonised with one of the deepest chords in the composition of the Aryan race—the universal, ancient, and persistent worship of the powers and forces of nature.

The chaos resulting from the break-up of the Western Empire being reduced to order mainly by the action of the Christian Church, at a period when the early germs of natural science had withered under the influence of the barbarian invasions, considerations relating to the next world occupied all mental activity not directly employed in ministering to the immediate and most pressing wants of this.

The art of the Middle Ages exhibits, as it were, the petrified embodiment of this spirit. Not only cathedral, church, chapel, religious-house, and parsonage were adorned with religious symbols and imagery, but such

---

* See "The Study of Sociology," chapters viii. to xii.

imagery all but as exclusively decorated the cottage, the palace, and the market-place. The purity of Christian morality had accidentally resulted in the banishment of the nude, and the vigour and perseverance with which the strongest natures and the acutest intellects devoted themselves to philosophy bore an inverse ratio to the energy with which traditional physics were almost unprofitably cultivated.

It is no difficult matter even now to realise the joyousness, the feeling of relief with which many minds must have hailed the first blossoming of that sweet artistic spring—the early Renaissance. Soon on each edifice, as if struck by a magic wand, every decorative detail, every niche and pinnacle blossoms out with a new life spreading over the architectural masses (the masses, as in St. Eustache, of Paris, still continuing as before), disguising them as some fair creeper may seem to replace the proper foliage of the tree it clasps.

To appreciate the delicacy and refinement, the full charm of the great movement architecturally, we must seek it in the land of its birth—in Italy, where the Certosa of Pavia, that dream of beauty, presents us with perhaps its most perfect expression—still essentially belonging to mediæval Christian art, yet modified by the movement to come,—a maiden with the blush of an approaching revelation, Margaret for the first time essaying Faust's fatal offering of pearls.

This artistic revolution, the changed aspect of church and oratory, must have reacted on and intensified the very movement which that change expressed. But if a mere modification in the architecture of cities had a tendency to modify men's minds, how much stronger must have been the effect of changed views as to the architecture of the universe (terrestrial and cosmical) induced by geographical, physical, and astronomical discovery!

The discovery of the New World has already been adverted to, and certainly no augmentation of knowledge in our own day—not even the revelations of spectrum analysis—can have had an effect nearly so startling. Yet even the shock of this geographical revelation must have been inferior in degree to that imparted by the uplifting of the solid earth from its foundations, and the casting of it forth from its proud physical supremacy to wander through space, a globe relatively insignificant,—effects which must have seemed to ensue in the minds of men when they first accepted heliocentric astronomy.

Yet later, when the full current of physical discovery had set in, and the disciples of Descartes and Bacon by diligent investigations and happily devised experiments were daily adding to the accumulated store of accurate knowledge in biology, in chemistry, and physics, the passionate pursuit of natural science grew by what it fed upon, and investigations which were begun, as alchemy and astrology, with utilitarian views only, were continued from pure love of and devotion to sciences which repaid persevering inquirers with responses definite, trustworthy, and capable of reiterated verification.

The transition which took place at the period of the Renaissance was a change from a social condition in which considerations relating to a future world still, at least apparently, predominated, to one revelling and exulting in physical nature and in this world as it offers itself spontaneously to our senses and our intellect. Such a change must have been like that which would be induced by passing from within some grand mediæval abbey church into a modern museum. Perhaps no man could, for the first time, so pass without unjustly depreciating the merits and the beauties of the one or of the other, so great seems at first the divergence between the spirits respectively embodied in those two manifestations.

Let us enter an old English abbey—Catherine of Arragon being still queen! The massive pillars of its nave, in long drawn series, have for five hundred years looked down on worshippers at the daily office. The successive styles of different portions of the fabric speak of the continued zeal for the beauty of God's house in successive generations of its cloistered inmates. Every window glows with colours artistically blended, revealing saintly forms. The light of day struggles in with difficulty, while here and there, in deeply shaded nooks, twinkling lamps burn before sacred images, and the shrine of the patron is brilliant with many tapers. On the walls may be seen the legend of his life, his temptations, martyrdom, and miracles. Above the rood, on the spectator's left, he sees depicted the joyful resurrection to a better life, while on his right the torments of the damned within the gaping "jaws of hell" are forcibly pourtrayed. As the monks give forth the *Magnificat* with sonorous chant, the incense rises before the lighted altar blazing with gold and jewels, and smell, in addition to sight and hearing, ministers to devotion. The daylight fades as, in the closing office of compline, the choir-boys' voices sing : "*In manus tuas, Domine, commendo spiritum meum,*" and the sweet "*Salve, Regina, Mater Misericordiæ*" peacefully dismisses the religious to their dormitory and the faithful to their homes. This world, its hopes and fears, its joys and sorrows, pale before the mind of one who thoroughly sympathises with such a scene; visions of holiness, of loving self-abnegation, of celestial beauty and divine love, rise up before him. Well may such a one, full of devout happiness, exclaim with heart and soul, "*Domine, dilexi decorem domus tuæ et locum habitationis gloriæ tuæ.*" A mind so influenced may at first tend to appreciate but faintly the merely natural creation, and feel but scanty reverence for its forces, and a qualified admiration for its beauties.

Let us now enter a modern museum. When its multitudinous contents have been so mastered that the intellect can grasp it as a whole, what a marvellous revelation of the physical universe it offers to the intellect attuned to its contemplation!

The organic and inorganic worlds combine to present to the duly instructed mind a vision of majesty and harmony undreamed of only two centuries ago.

In its geological section, even the tertiary fossiliferous rocks speak of an antiquity compared with which the pyramids of Egypt are but of yesterday. Majestic remains of vast creatures once living but now extinct exercise the mind in fruitful conjectures, which mentally bring back forms passed away for ever to live again for the wonder and delight of the votaries of science. The crystalline minerals reveal innate laws of symmetry and beauty, which, as it were, lend a sort of life even to inorganic nature.

In the section devoted to the illustration of the organic world as it lives around us now, we may note the harmonious organisation (so fitted to its needs) of each species of animal and plant, proclaiming a nature instinct with intelligence as well as with beauty. Here also we may learn how slight differences of colour or form may protect the individual life, and what fatal effects may ensue from an apparently trifling defect of structure. Teeming nature is seen to be the mother of myriads of creatures of which but few can reach maturity, and seems to proclaim trumpet-tongued a natural gospel of happiness for the healthy, the beautiful, the strong.

Introductory. 21

The loveliest tints displayed by birds as well as their springtide melody, the blossom of all flowers as well as their sweetest perfumes, all become known to us as but subordinate agencies ministering to the great reproductive function—spontaneous tributes of organic life to Alma Venus. Such phenomena seem to combine with the evidences of the destructive and apparently cruel processes of nature to inculcate the brief lesson of the grim symbol at the Egyptian festival—" Enjoy."

But in our temple of nature it is not only the creatures of this planet which offer themselves to our scrutiny, but even portions of other spheres; and meteorolites prove to us that similar substances and similar laws to those existing on this earth pervade regions of space remote from and inaccessible to us.

How strongly does a nature so replete with interest, with wonder, with beauty, with pleasure, and with awe, solicit the devotion of man's faculties! The courts of such a scientific temple tend to produce in not a few minds feelings of delight mingled with a quasi-religious sentiment; and when, instructed by such teaching, we wander forth amidst the living products of nature, that feeling becomes intensified indeed.

Tropical scenes full of exuberant organic life are, of course, best calculated to call it forth; but even in our own land there is ample material for evoking it.

When from some smooth-browed, chalky down we,

reposing amidst fragrant wild flowers and the hum of busy insect life, look down on the peaceful ocean rippling in sun-lit splendour at our feet, as we mark the sea-fowl sailing in circles with rarely flapping wing, or listen to the lark rising blithely through the summer air,—how strong with many will be the impulse towards a joyous cultus of an underlying soul of which such visible beauty is the living and palpitating garment! The great Pan lives once more, nor is Aphrodite unlikely to receive a mute and mental homage. This world is felt to be lovely and sweet indeed, and visions of exclusively terrestrial joy pass before the mind, and tend to produce in it scanty reverence for the forms and but slight admiration for the beauties of Christian supernaturalism.

It is in a sense which the foregoing comparison may serve to illustrate that the whole modern movement dating from the very first breath of the Renaissance may be regarded as being essentially a return towards paganism—not of course (at least in the first instance) to the worship of the old gods, but to much of the spirit which underlay that worship.

The essence of the paganism in Europe and Aryan Asia with which Christianity contended, did not consist in any definite credo, or in any exclusive cultus, else how could the strange gods of the East have found a home in the capital of the Roman empire? The essence of that paganism was, whatever may have been its remote origin, mainly pantheism, and consisted in a systematic contemplation of this world as it is, with a certain religiosity indeed, but without supernatural (as distinguished from preternatural) aspirations or the idea of holiness. Its religious conceptions were drawn from physical nature, reposed on natural phenomena, and taking such nature as she is, logically resulted in rites which answered both to her joyous and to her gloomy aspects. Moreover, the philosophy of the ancient pagan world was in this respect in harmony with its religion.

"It was from a physical point of view of the world, and a desire to reduce it to a physical unity, that Greek philosophy took its start; and the confusion of God with the world, as it was involved in its beginning, so remains its great error during the course of nine hundred years, from Thales to Plotinus. In the seventh century before Christ, the wise men of Greece all proceeded from the expressed or the tacit assumption of one world-forming force, whether they considered this as bound up with matter or as severed from it, whether they called it nature or the divine, or by any other name. This conception forms the common basis of the mechanical doctrine of nature on the one hand, and of the dynamical doctrine of nature on the other. All the various schools of materialistic pantheism, of which the Ionic is the first, spring from the former; all the various schools of idealistic pantheism, of which the Eleatic is the first, spring from the latter. In the former the confusion of God with the world consists in making Him its material cause; in the latter it consists in making Him its formal cause: in both, the relation of all existing things to Him is that of the appearance to the essence, that of the part to the whole." *

Before the advent of Christianity the worship of nature had for untold ages entered into the very marrow of the bones of our forefathers. The Christian Church, in spite of its apparent mediæval triumph, had on the masses but an imperfect hold, and in some countries had but the acceptance of a brief tradition from fathers on whom it had been imposed by the sword a few centuries before. What wonder then if, under the influences brought to bear since the year 1500, Christianity is becoming disintegrated over wide areas, and the old pagan sentiment reappearing like some old classical poem on the surface of a palimpsest from which the later mediæval superscriptions are being removed!

As to the Renaissance, even its sympathetic historian, Mr. W. H. Pater, observes: "One of the strongest characteristics of that outbreak . . . was its antinomianism, its spirit of rebellion and revolt against the moral and religious ideas of the age. In their search after the pleasures of the senses and the imagination, in their care

---

* T. W. Allies, " Formation of Christendom," part iii., p. 363.

for beauty, in their worship of the body, people were impelled beyond the bounds of the primitive Christian ideal; and their love became a strange idolatry, a strange rival religion. It was the return of that ancient Venus, not dead, but only hidden for a time in the caves of the Venusberg, of those old pagan gods still going to and fro on the earth, under all sorts of disguises."*

It is then here contended that the whole modern movement from the humanists of the Renaissance to the present day has been and is a pagan revival; the reappearance of a passionate love for and a desire to rest in and thoroughly sympathise with mere nature, accompanied by a more or less complete and sympathetic rejection of the supernatural, its aspirations, its consolations, and its terrors.

But to this position at least two objections may be made. First, it may be said that many sincere and thorough Christians have been profoundly imbued with a love of nature, as was especially the case with the seraphic father, the great St. Francis. Secondly, it may be objected that the modern period has been largely religious, and that the movement of the Reformation has been here unjustly and unreasonably ignored.

To the first objection it may be replied, there are two ways of loving and regarding nature.

St. Francis, the tenderly beloved and unspeakably

---

* "Studies in the History of the Renaissance." By Walter H. Pater, Fellow of Brasenose College, Oxford.

revered father of so many saintly followers—he who was deservedly called an *alter Christus*—was indeed a lover of nature; and, as we read in his life, the creatures of the forest recognised and responded to his love by familiar approach and ready obedience: however, he always loved the creature in and for the Creator; he would address the insect as "brother fly," recognising in it an inferior created image of the same personal God whose chosen servant he was. The divinity he worshipped was no pantheistic soul in nature, but one who was his king as well as He in whom all things had their being. For whole days kneeling in devout contemplation, with tears of love he would again and again repeat with fond iteration the words, "*Rex meus et Deus meus,*" as well as, "*Deus meus et omnia.*"

Such love of nature is profoundly Christian, and thoroughly antagonistic to that love of it for its own sake simply, which is as profoundly pagan. In so far as our modern poets and other artists partake of this Franciscan spirit, in so far are they in harmony at once with nature and with Christianity. But there is little doubt that the prevailing tone of sentiment has long been increasingly pagan, until its most hideous features reveal themselves in a living English poet, by open revilings of Christianity, amidst loathsome and revoltingly filthy verses, which seem to invoke a combined worship of the old deities of lust and cruelty.

Introductory. 27

But even the most innocent and refined minds show, as might be expected, the influence of the prevailing spirit, and pantheism exhales from the pure lines of Wordsworth, as from the endless painted repetitions of wood and water, moor and sea, which line the walls of our annual exhibitions.

As to the second supposed objection, it may be observed in reply to it, that in the movement of the Reformation two distinct currents are manifest.

One of these flowed in harmony with that previously initiated by the humanists, as its effects on the Church were simply disintegrating. In so far as it tended more or less completely to the negation of Christianity, it certainly aided the great pagan revival, and may justly claim a place of distinction amidst the agents of such restoration.

But the other current is that with which good people in this country associate the Reformation—that, namely, by which certain remnants of dogma were drifted together in definite but unstable aggregations, labelled "Lutheranism," "Calvinism," and what not.

But this second current was a mere "backwater," and has resulted in no developments. The materials it stranded have remained stationary, or, as in Switzerland and Prussia, have utterly disintegrated, falling into and directly aiding to give impetus to the great stream of the naturalistic pagan revival. We may not unreasonably suspect that had Luther foreseen the ultimate outcome of his Biblical criticisms he would have shrunk back into his cloister and refused to aid a movement which had in no way his sympathy.

A recent writer in the *Times* has graphically pourtrayed the present state of Protestantism in Germany. He tells us: " Young men decline to ascend the pulpit. Already many parsonages are empty, and more are becoming so every day. To illustrate this astonishing fact by a few figures : the eight Prussian universities in 1831 boasted 2203 theological students; by the winter of 1873 this figure has dwindled down to 740. Nor does it look more promising in western and southern Germany. Of the two Hessian universities of Marburg and Giessen, the former had 124 theological students in 1831, against 46 in 1873; the latter having 80 in 1850, against 10 in 1873. Even in Würtemberg, the most theologically inclined region of Germany, the supply of young candidates for clerical honours has so steadily diminished, that whereas 48 were examined in 1823, only 32 were in 1873. But what is more significant than anything else is, that of the Prussian students of theology who matriculated in the Prussian universities between 1851 and 1873, one third abandoned theology before ordination."

Dogmatic Protestantism, as such, is essentially anti-scientific and profoundly anti-naturalistic, proclaiming as it does, the utter depravity and helplessness of our human nature, and M. de Candolle* has recently shown how Geneva has gained its scientific eminence only since it threw off its orthodox Protestant character.

It may be affirmed then that Protestantism, *as* Protestantism, has had no *positive* effect, and therefore has no true place in the great humanistic naturalistic revival, in spite of the vigorous self-reliance and generous nobility of character so widely prevalent in much of the area it occupies. Its direct effects have been but negative, and it has only aided that revival in so far as it has accelerated the process of Christian disintegration.

We may now turn our attention to yet another aspect in which the movement of the last three centuries may be regarded; namely, its political effects.

In the pagan Roman Empire, as before in Greece, the omnipotence of the State was a recognised as well as a logical doctrine. Religion, though polytheistic, was pantheistic, as the philosophy was prevalently monistic. The individual citizen had no sacred god-given rights to maintain, and the will or the welfare of the community rose superior to every plea which any single citizen could put forward.

It was the Jews and Christians, with a religion reposing on a dualistic philosophy, who, for the first time, to the amazement of judges who would fain have been

---

* " Histoire des Savants depuis deux Siècles," par A. de Candolle : Genève, 1873.

merciful, maintained the sacred rights of conscience, and by patient endurance, sufferings, and death, vindicated the claim of each individual—not only citizen, but slave—to the freedom of a rational and responsible nature.

As the mediæval Christendom was slowly built up, not only did the rights of conscience, under the shelter and sanction of the Church, find constant recognition, but civil privileges and immunities were gained from rude feudal lords as consequences of such rights.

The Christian Church ever officially respected the rights of conscience, and however much such rights were practically disregarded in Spain or elsewhere, never claimed jurisdiction over any but her own spiritual children; that is, the baptized. Jews were ever protected at Rome, and long met with a shelter there denied them in almost the whole of Christendom besides. Unlike Mahometanism, the Church never sanctioned the use of the sword for the propagation of the faith, though asserting the legitimacy of its use for purposes of defence.

Especially was the Church watchful against the assertion of religious authority or control on the part of the State. The religious authorities were the representatives of the people who believed in and accepted their ministrations, and submitted to them their consciences, and thus our own great and glorious martyr of Canterbury, the pride of the English Church, died for liberty of conscience, for liberty in religion, of the people's chosen guides against the would-be autocracy of a king who sought to lord it over the consciences as well as over the bodies of his subjects.

Coincidentally with the first breath of the humanistic spirit, and increasing with the movement of the Renaissance, appeared a revival of State claims over the individual consciences of subjects, and when the destructive portion of the Reformation movement had done its work, it left behind it, as a worthy monument, that monstrous rule of German legislation, "*Cujus regio ejus religio*," and paganism reappeared in the political arena.

Religious indifferentism and the rapid multiplication of sects in certain countries have for a time suspended the practical development of this worst of tyrannies; but in *theory* the evil has augmented, and is in our own day beginning to bear bitter practical fruit in Germany and Switzerland.

It has augmented theoretically, because the religious tyranny of the sixteenth and seventeenth centuries was at least avowedly based on an assertion of religious truth and a professed care for the souls of subjects. Now, however, we meet with an express negation of such motives, and the naked assertion of the State's right, *qua* State, to dictate to its subjects their religious practices and impose on them its own doctrines—the logical outcome of the monistic philosophy in vogue.

Christians have again imposed upon them the glorious

task of maintaining by self-denial and suffering the common rights of all men and the most fundamental and sacred of all liberties—the liberty to adhere with undeviating fidelity, in speech and action as well as in thought, to what they believe to be truth revealed to them by their Creator.

The supreme and indefeasible rights of conscience have never perhaps been more admirably defended than by the most widely venerated priest of our own time and country, Father Newman.* He tells us:—

"The rule and measure of duty is not utility, nor expedience, nor the happiness of the greatest number, nor State convenience, nor fitness, order, and the *pulchrum*. Conscience is not a long-sighted selfishness, nor a desire to be consistent with oneself; but it is a message from Him, who, both in nature and in grace, speaks to us behind a veil, and teaches and rules us by His representatives. Conscience is the aboriginal vicar of Christ, a prophet in its informations, a monarch in its peremptoriness, a priest in its blessings and anathemas, and, even though the eternal priesthood throughout the Church should cease to be, in it the sacerdotal principle would remain and would have sway."

As to the necessary relation of the visible head of the Church to the claims of conscience, and the certainty

---

* See his "Letter to the Duke of Norfolk," p. 57.

that in him they must find a defender, he adds: "Did the pope speak against conscience in the true sense of the word, he would commit a suicidal act. He would be cutting the ground from under his feet. His very mission is to proclaim the moral law, and to protect and strengthen that light which enlighteneth every man that cometh into the world."

On the law of conscience and its sacredness are founded both his authority in theory and his power in fact: "The championship of the moral law and of the conscience is his *raison d'être*. The fact of his mission is the answer to the complaints of those who feel the insufficiency of the natural light; and the insufficiency of that light is the justification of his mission."

That in his view as to the paramount claims of conscience he is but following the traditions and authorities of the Church he makes plain by references and quotations. After quoting the judgment, "He who acts against conscience loses his soul," adduced from the fourth Lateran council by Cardinal Gousset, he adds: "This dictum is brought out with singular fulness and force in the moral treatises of theologians. The celebrated school known as the Salmanticenses, or Carmelites of Salamanca, lays down the broad proposition, that conscience is ever to be obeyed, whether it tells us truly or erroneously, and that, whether the error is the fault of the person thus erring or not. They say that this opinion is certain, and refer, as agreeing with them, to St. Thomas, St. Bonaventura, Cajetan, Vasquez, Durandus, Navarrus, Corduba, Layman, Escobar, and fourteen others. Two of them even say this opinion is *de fide*."

He also quotes Busenbaum, of the Society of Jesus, as saying : " A heretic, as long as he judges his sect to be more or equally deserving of belief, has no obligation to believe (in the Church) ; " and, "when men who have been brought up in heresy are persuaded from boyhood that we impugn and attack the word of God, that we are idolaters, pestilent deceivers, and therefore are to be shunned as pestilences, they cannot, while this persuasion lasts, with a safe conscience hear us."

Again, he cites Antonio Corduba, a Spanish Franciscan, as stating the doctrine yet more pointedly, and saying : "In no manner is it lawful to act against conscience, even though a law, or a superior commands it." —*De Conscient.*, p. 138.

Finally, he quotes the French Dominican Natalis Alexander, as declaring that "if in the judgment of conscience, though a mistaken conscience, a man is persuaded that what his superior commands is displeasing to God, he is bound not to obey." *Théol., tome* ii., p. 32.

Such a power then as the Christian Church must ever be the most efficient and unflinching upholder of the greatest and the noblest of the rights of man.

We come now to the third question : What is likely

to be the further effect of this revived pagan spirit, and is it likely henceforward to advance or to recede?

It is manifest at once that no one should venture to apply himself to the solution of this problem without great diffidence and an exceptionally earnest desire and determination to render scrupulous justice to views which he does not share, and to assign full weight to forces and tendencies, the actions of which conflict with his own personal desires and inspirations.

Certain classes of persons also are plainly disqualified from forming in this matter an opinion deserving any serious attention.

Thus no one can estimate the action of the opposing forces who has not entered into and more or less sympathetically made his own the spirit which animates each.

For example, no one is qualified who does not really understand Christianity, who does not comprehend what developments are really congruous with it, or accepts the crude and shallow views so widely prevalent on the subject.

Similarly, no one is qualified who does not possess, not only a certain scientific culture, but also a mind capable of feeling sympathy with, and pleasure at, every advance of physical discovery.

Such an inquirer should have both the theological and the anti-theological bias reduced to a minimum degree, and be capable of taking a broad view of every speculative question.

Thus no one nurtured in a narrow school of theology, and persisting to mature life in that position, can hope to attain an accurate view of the position; and the same may be said of any one trained in a narrow physical school, or who, with the *naïveté* of Professor Huxley, thinks, apparently, to destroy Christianity from the platform of physical science.

Mr. Herbert Spencer possesses qualities enabling him to grapple such a problem with vigour and success, and it is matter of deep regret that he has not thought it worth while to qualify himself for the congenial task by a preliminary knowledge of Christianity. It is not of course meant to imply that he does not possess the ordinary information with regard to it common to all men of education in this country. Such information, however, is quite insufficient for the purpose, and surely far more than this might be expected from Mr. Herbert Spencer. As a fact, however, he gives no evidence of having acquainted himself with Christian philosophy, or with the doctrines, precepts, and counsels of the Christian Church, and yet it cannot be denied that that institution has occupied and still occupies no inconsiderable or uninfluential place amongst the factors of social evolution. But Mr. Spencer has more or less distinctly declared himself in this matter, and the wide acceptance which his philosophy has attained on both sides of the Atlantic renders it a matter of interest to inquire into the possible future of that philosophy, in connection with the future course of the great pagan revival.

It is by no means improbable that such revival may be carried on to a far greater development than it has yet attained, and assume a far more distinctly religious aspect.

The human mind will never rest in the mere materialism of Strauss, or in the inane worship of abstract humanity devised by Comte.

Mr. Spencer himself well remarks* concerning religion, that the belief that its "object-matter can be replaced by another object-matter, as supposed by those who think the 'Religion of Humanity' will be the religion of the future, is a belief countenanced neither by induction nor by deduction. However dominant may become the moral sentiment enlisted on behalf of humanity, it can never exclude the sentiment, alone properly religious, awakened by that which is behind humanity and behind all other things. . . . No such thing as a 'Religion of Humanity' can ever do more than temporarily shut out the thought of a Power of which humanity is but a small and fugitive product—which was in course of ever-changing manifestation before humanity was, and will continue

---

* "The Study of Sociology," p. 311.

through other manifestations when humanity has ceased to be."

In connection with workings of and self-devotion to merely an abstract humanity, the following words of Mr. Mott* may be quoted with advantage :—

"The hope of progress, to have any powerful influence upon us, must be the hope of something in which we ourselves, or those who are really dear to us, can share; not the hope that a higher race of beings will inhabit the earth long after we have done with it. If I heard that the Emperor of China was a much better and nobler being than myself, I do not feel that I should be much elated by the news. Even if I congratulated himself and his subjects, my personal feelings would be rather grim. In like manner, the knowledge that my own lot, and the lot of those I love, was a very miserable one compared with what my descendants would inherit a thousand years hence, could not give me a very cheerful view of life in general. Nor is there any selfishness in this, for selfishness does not consist in highly valuing our own happiness —this is surely what the angels do—but in being willing to sacrifice the happiness of others in order to secure our own.

"The hope of improving the condition of others in whom our affections are interested is indeed one of the

---

* See "Origin of Savage Life," p. 43.

highest motives for exertion; but to suppose that we can carry such affection forward to far distant generations is to misinterpret human nature. The feeling which is mistaken for such transcendental love is a sentimental product of the imagination, which seeks to render the hope of individual immortality unnecessary to our happiness, by persuading us to forget the individual and to think only of the race. The feeling is false to nature, and can never be a real power in the world."

But if we may expect the evolution of a non-Christian religiosity in harmony more or less with the wants and nature of man as we find him, in what direction may we look for such development? The deliberate invention of a new religion has been experimentally demonstrated to be a hopeless task, and the age of myth-spinning has gone by in cultivated Europe and America.

It is not impossible, however, that a new pagan cultus may, should its need be felt, be one day evolved in connection with the philosophy of Mr. Spencer himself.

It is evident that such an evolution is possible, since Mr. Spencer is indeed essentially a Brahman, and his creed Brahmanism, potentially containing a whole pantheon of cosmical divinities, the worship of which is not incapable of being justified to the reason and conscience of many of such as really accept his philosophy. For Mr. Spencer is never tired of telling us that everything is some form of the Unknowable, while of this First Cause Itself we must predicate nothing save bare existence; to attribute to it even intelligence and will would be, according to him, to speak derogatively of it.

Now, in Brahmanism, "Para-Brahm" "is literally an unknown God. He has no qualities, no attributes, no activity. He is neither the object of hope, fear, love, nor aversion."*

We read in the *Upanishad* as follows: "How can anyone teach concerning Brahma? He is neither the Known nor the Unknown. That which cannot be expressed by words, but through which all expression comes, this I know to be Brahma. That which cannot be thought by the mind, but by which all thinking comes, this I know is Brahma. That which cannot be seen by the eye, but by which the eye sees, is Brahma. If thou thinkest that thou canst know it, then in truth thou knowest it very little. To whom it is unknown he knows it; but to whom it is known, he knows it not. . . . One cannot attain to it through the word, through the mind, or through the eye. It is only reached by him who says, 'It is!' 'It is!'"†

Surely if the doctrine of metempsychosis were true, Mr. Spencer must be no other than the author of the *Upanishad* himself reappearing in the nineteenth century!

---

* See James Freeman Clarke's "Ten Great Religions." Trübner: 1871, p. 84.

† Op. cit., p. 117.

The passage quoted harmonises remarkably with the teaching of our English philosopher, who is no decrier of religion, but as we have seen, postulates the necessity of its existence, however modified its forms, as long as humanity endures.

But if such views of the First Cause ever become generally diffused and popular in a country in which the instinct of worship is strong, and accompanied by a cultivated taste sure to develop itself in a more or less elaborate ritual, a strange result would not be far off.

All things, beauty, light, sound, morality, love, justice, etc., are modes of the Unknowable—forms of Brahma. The Unknowable cannot be thought, but Its *modes* can, and they are worthy of reverence, because they are Its modes.

Mr. Spencer complains that the reverence Christians show to God is unworthy, does not properly express the extreme awe and reverence due to the Unknowable.

But the Unknowable, though not an object of direct worship, may be—nay, should be—worshipped in and through Its modes.

Thus we come to a God of beauty, a God of light, a God of harmony, etc., each being a form of the Unknowable, and worthy of separate worship.

But this worship should be quite unlike that which the Christian Church everywhere pays to its canonised members, since the subordination of these latter is fully recognised and their intercession alone sought. But the modes of the Unknowable would not be subordinate, would not be mere creatures to intercede, but co-equal and independent powers, one with that of which they are modes, and therefore divine. In other words, we have at once a restored polytheism.*

And indeed, in the absence of revelation, what more worthy symbol of beneficent modes of the Unknowable could be selected for an object of worship than the sun? Science teaches us that it is, in fact, not only the agent by which the material world around us is clothed in beauty and in joy, but even that by which alone beauty, goodness, and truth themselves are manifested to us.

For its worship some revival of antique rites might be gradually engrafted on existing forms—for the principle of continuity must be recognised and acted on—while

---

* "Absolute unity admits into its capacious bosom all gods, for the gods so admitted are simply parts of one universal power, which is the substance of all things. Pantheism and polytheism share the same error of giving this incommunicable Name to stocks and stones; for if the being of God is the being of all things, it is as true to say a stone is God, as to say a stone is a being. If God be at once the matter and the soul of the world, and in both, in spite of His eternity and unchangeableness, be subject to every change in time, the idolaters were not to be blamed for honouring with divine worship the air or the fire or irrational animals; rather, the only blame they deserved was that they did not worship everything."—Allies' "Formation of Christendom," part iii., p. 370.

glowing passages from the works of Professor Tyndall may well supply antiphons and suggest hymns for its ritual.

Hereafter, then, in the worship of the First Cause, not as made known to us by His own act of voluntary self revelation, but as manifested in the material world alone, we may find a fuller development of that pagan revival, which for more than three centuries has been gathering life and energy. But we shall not yet have reached its culmination.

To be logical, we must not ignore *any* side of nature, which is equally in every aspect a mode of the Unknowable. If acts prompted by the devotion of a mother's love are to be reverently recognised as one mode of that which alone IS, not one bit less is the traffic of the courtesan another such mode; and if the chastisement of the assassin may claim ITS sanction, so the assassin may also equally claim it for the act on account of which he is chastised.

The Christianity which yet remains diffused amongst us, and the refinement of modern manners, render the open practice of licentious and sanguinary rites as yet impossible, but the spirit which prompted them finds in this system its complete and logical justification, as it has found in a contemporary poet its distinct lyrical expression. The tendency of the movement is to approach little by little towards this worst phase of paganism, as the corruption of morals gradually increases, through the temporarily decreasing influence of Christianity upon the outer surface of society.

Already we hear openly advocated the murder of the unborn, the sick, the suffering, and the old, as well as self-murder. Free love has not only its advocates, but its avowed votaries, and a hatred of marriage and the family is one of the sentiments common to those political enthusiasts who claim for themselves, *par excellence*, the title of "advanced."

When such views come to be mastered and accepted by many of those who adopt the religious system here sketched, they will doubtless powerfully reinforce, but also strongly affect the religious system itself—possibly even its ritualistic expression. Thus the revived paganism of the future may be calculated to startle the rationalist of to-day fully as much as the revived paganism of to-day would have startled a reformer of the time of Luther.

It remains to consider the effect on Christianity of the further development of the great movement we now witness, and to endeavour to predict the result of the renewed conflict between such a modified Christianity and a so revived paganism.

CHAPTER II.

POLITICAL EVOLUTION.

IN the first chapter of this essay an endeavour was made to investigate the meaning and tendency of that great process of social change which has been going on since the thirteenth century, and which still continues.

This process was explained as a prolonged struggle between the mediæval theocracy and a reviving paganism,* the latter succeeding in more and more thoroughly rejecting the domination which at an early period the

---

* In the valuable and interesting essay by the Rev. A. M. Fairbairn, which appeared in the number of the *Contemporary Review* for October, 1873, views are put forward singularly harmonising with those above referred to. The religious belief prevailing in Europe is represented by him as being a synthesis of Hebraistic and Hellenistic elements (p. 806), and it is shown how the old, pre-Christian " Indo-European mode of conceiving and expressing Deity is in almost every respect a contrast to the Semitic. The general terms" in Indo-European religions " were primarily expressive of physical qualities" (p. 797), and " all the Indo-European religions bear the stamp of this primitive naturalism" (p. 799). By the pagan revival spoken of in the first chapter was meant an increasing action expulsive of the Hebraistic elements, and the " paganism" referred to is equivalent to the Indo-European " naturalism" of Mr. Fairbairn, with its degraded conceptions of God, its divorce between religion and ethics, its state absolutism, and the slavery of the individual conscience.

former had obtained. The anticipation was also expressed that this repudiation would be carried to a much further point than it has as yet reached.

The consideration of two questions was declared to be a desideratum. These were—

(1) The "*effect on Christianity of the further development of the great movement.*"

(2) The probable "*result of the renewed conflict between such a modified Christianity and a so revived paganism.*"

It was, however, by anticipation, observed that it was necessary to the successful consideration of these questions, that the "inquirer should have both the theological and the anti-theological bias reduced to a minimum degree," but that he should at the same time know "what developments are really congruous with Christianity," since without such knowledge it must be manifestly impossible for him to judge of the effects of Contemporary Evolution upon it.

Before proceeding to attempt the solution of the two grave problems which are here to occupy us, it may be remarked that the question as to the *truth of Christianity* is here left entirely on one side, the obvious or admitted tendencies of known natural forces and laws being alone taken into consideration.

Assuming that "paganism" or "Aryan naturalism" is playing the great part here assigned to it, and is likely to produce yet greater effects in the future, it is manifest that Christianity must be thus profoundly modified or entirely destroyed, unless it contains latent powers and capacities calculated to meet such attacks and provide for such trials. If, however, Christianity does contain such powers in a high degree, it is evident that resurging paganism may but be the occasion for the outward manifestation of such latent capacities, and that to its hostile action Christianity may be indebted for the most startling and prodigious of its triumphs.

To investigate, then, the question whether Christianity is likely to be utterly destroyed, or more or less enfeebled, or slightly or greatly strengthened by the further development of the naturalistic movement, we must examine that movement in its (1) POLITICAL, (2) SCIENTIFIC, and (3) PHILOSOPHIC aspects.

The questions of the effects of contemporary scientific and philosophic evolution on Christianity may be deferred to succeeding chapters. Here it is proposed to consider CHRISTIANITY AND POLITICAL EVOLUTION only.

Some of the political effects of the further development, in our own day and hereafter, of the humanistic Renaissance were briefly indicated in the first chapter,* but as a necessary groundwork for estimating the future, it will be well here to begin with a somewhat fuller though brief survey of past and present socio-political changes.

---

* Page 29.

At the period of Innocent III., the Christian theocracy in Europe had proximately attained its greatest actual development.

The social institutions and whole political fabric avowedly reposed upon an all but universally accepted divine authority, and upon a revelation the declarations of which were interpreted and systematically applied to all circumstances as they arose by spiritual authorities recognised as the revealed system's God-appointed administrators, of whom one supreme pontiff was the acknowledged head.

The Christian political system having thus temporarily organised itself and grown up into this near approach to a universal theocracy, began slowly to disintegrate.

Incipiently resurging paganism first showed itself politically in a spirit of religious "nationalism" opposing itself to the cosmopolitan religious conception embodied in the papacy. Paganism was especially national, and the principle of "nationalism" in religion when once introduced into Christendom by legislative impediments to the free exercise of the Christian central and controlling power, rapidly developed itself and expanded fatally to the Christian theocracy.

In France that "eldest son of the Church," Philip the Fair, dealt the first great blow to the Christian political system in the persons of Boniface VIII. and the Knight Templars. Thenceforward the anti-theocratic spirit manifested itself now and again in opposition to the Church, and when this action was apparently reversed by the royal protection extended to Christianity against the revolt of Luther and Calvin, it was in reality but intensified by a surrender of control in spiritual things as a return for such protection.

The cessation of the subsequent religious troubles through the accession of the politic Henry IV. was the occasion of the yet further domination of the Church by the State, culminating in the despotism of Louis XIV., who avowed himself as not only resuming in his own person the whole civil power of the State, but as the God-giver and sacred Vicegerent of Deity, against whose will *no* right, whether of privilege, property, or conscience, should under any circumstances assert itself.

The wide divergence of such a social system from the old mediæval theocracy is patent enough, nevertheless that system continued to exhibit a considerable deference to older forms, and attempted to constitute a sort of national theocracy of its own, founded on the king's "divine right."

The leprous regency and the crowned infamy which succeeded could not however but greatly weaken the force of the alleged supernatural authority of the royal autocracy, which authority was at the same time further enfeebled by the advance of the "philosophic" spirit.

Thus, before the unhappy Louis XVI. opened the

States-General, he had come to be regarded by an influential part of the nation as merely *its* representative, and "divine right," so far as recognised at all, had passed to the nation as a whole. Nevertheless, the old laws continuing still, gave him power over the consciences of his subjects in the form of State control of the French Church.

When the sovereignty of the French people through representatives—or those who asserted themselves to be the representatives of such representatives—succeeded to the royal power in the state, they not unnaturally assumed and exaggerated that ecclesiastical supremacy which had been conceded to the monarch, and the "civil constitution of the clergy" was the result. Thus the singular anomaly presented itself of one section of citizens claiming to dispose of the consciences of their fellow-citizens by imposing what was in fact a new State religion in the name of *liberty*.

It is plain then that the diminution and destruction of the royal power, instead of reversing the current which had accompanied its augmentation, actually intensified it.

Still, as long as any profession of religion remained, there was always at least a nominal and professed respect for liberty and conscience; but it is interesting to note that the extreme of intolerance and persecution attended the proclaimed atheism of Hebert and the Commune.

In the rise of what afterwards became "imperialism," that most cynical and unscrupulous of tyrants the first Napoleon availed himself of the rising tide in favour of freedom of conscience to legislate for the restoration and support of the French Church, and here some historical students might suspect that we encounter a real theocratic reaction. Such a suspicion, however, would be groundless. Not upon the old basis of "revelation," but on that of the common rights of different religions to the support of an indifferent State, was the re-establishment effected, and while the lay power thus asserted its supremacy and independence more than even under the old kings, privileges conceded to the really Christian monarchs were retained by the man whose treatment of Pius VII. proclaimed at once his paganism and his brutality.

The Restoration did, indeed, more or less ally itself with the strong desire entertained by an influential portion of the nation for a reversion in the theocratic direction, especially under Charles X., with speedy loss of his throne as a result. Nevertheless, that even this monarch was animated by the prevailing anti-theocratic spirit is shown by that expulsion of the Jesuits which so shortly preceded his own exile.

During the reign of the "citizen king," theocratic tendencies were notoriously in disfavour; while under Napoleon III., and through his act, the mediæval theocracy of Christendom has received its supreme blow in the revolutionising of Italy, with loss to the pope of his civil princedom as a result.

The last hopes of those in France or elsewhere who sigh for the re-elevation of the tattered and disfigured banner of the mediæval Christian theocracy have long centred in the Count de Chambord. But the head of that government which lately seemed so near accomplishing his elevation to the throne disclaimed in distinct and memorable words, in the name of his party and of the French clergy, any desire for mediæval reaction, and the Count de Chambord himself has accepted liberty of conscience, freedom of worship, and the other articles of modern constitutionalism; so that his accession, if it were even possible, could not have any other effect than that of lending to modern civicism the halo of his legitimacy.

The mediæval Christian theocracy, then, in France may be said to be definitively at an end, and attacks on freedom and conscience are to be apprehended from the friends and favourers of communistic fanaticism alone.

In England a parallel series of changes has been differently effected.

Henry VIII. (that incarnation of the dominant English spirit of his time) completed by his despotism a process which had been gradually developing itself in preceding reigns by the formal absorption of ecclesiastical authority in the person of the king, made "Head of the Church."

But the theocracy in England, though thus changed as to its base, far from being overthrown, was for a time augmented, and it was not until after it had transformed itself into the despotism of the Commonwealth, that its vigour began slowly to relax. The very slowness was, however, one cause of the continuity of its ebb, for the resistance of the Protestant bishops to the tyranny of James II. (itself sustained by the theocratic sentiment) powerfully aided in bringing about the expulsion of one who, had he unhappily remained, might have effected a strongly reactionary transformation.

The government of the Dutchman, with its terrible penal laws, was despotic enough; but its tendencies were distinctly anti-theocratic, and such thenceforward has been the general direction of our legislation.

Nevertheless, so conservative are we, that to this day the Christian theocracy remains exceptionally erect in England. We have, not only a national Church still in possession of its territorial endowments, but a multitude of our positive enactments (such as those respecting the observance of Sunday) repose on a more or less distinct theocratic basis, as also do our conspicuous state ceremonials, from the coronation of the chief magistrate downwards.

There can be little doubt, however, but that these last relics will, more or less, gradually disappear. In spite of the apparent present strength of Conservatism, converging efforts from most opposite sides threaten that last venerable mediæval relic irreverently termed by the late Dr. Wilberforce the "Squarson."

If we turn to Spain we find there is a very interesting and instructive example of the same process under very different forms and with very different results. The prolonged Moorish wars caused Christianity to entwine itself so intimately with the Spanish social structure, that the mediæval theocracy remained in full force to the end of the reign of the great Isabella. Nevertheless it was taking a peculiar direction, not found in other countries in Europe.

As elsewhere, so also in Spain, the monarch came to share in that exaggerated authority and dignity which kings acquired, in the sixteenth century, as the patrons or as the vanquishers of the Church within their borders. But in Spain the monarch had to share his power with another for a time co-ordinate, independent, and invincible authority—the frightful Spanish Inquisition.

This institution, which originally, indeed, took its rise in a development of the official Christian system, soon became so powerful, owing to local conditions, as to be able to defy and successfully resist that theocracy in which it took its rise, and the singular spectacle presented itself of a power professing to have for its one object the complete and minute enforcement of Church authority itself refusing to obey the supreme head of the very Church it professed to serve.

Overshadowing and obscuring both royal and papal authority, this monstrous Christian parasite offered a peculiar obstacle to overt manifestations of reviving paganism, although itself hostile to the true theocratic spirit. That it was not the true representative of the latter was shown by the unerring instinct of resurging paganism, which first expelled, not the inquisitors, but their occasional victims the Jesuits—ever in closest and most sympathetic union with the head of Christendom.

Again, the anti-theocratic changes in Spain were mainly brought about by foreign influences. So that small tentative returns towards some of the old laws and practices were, as being national, more or less popular and practicable, down almost to 1868.

The extremely radical measures which were for a time adopted show that the forcible repression of the anti-theocratic movement in Spain has in the end but intensified its action, and given rise to a spirit of antagonistic fanaticism akin to, if not in excess of, that of the Parisian Commune.

But few fragments of the Christian theocracy remain in the Madrid Government of Spain to-day, even under King Alfonso; but many hope or fear that a return to that theocracy may be effected under the sovereignty of " Charles VII." Some of those, however, who are personally acquainted with " His Most Catholic Majesty," positively affirm that nothing is farther from his thoughts or intentions than the re-introduction of mediæval theocracy into Spain, —earnest as he is said to be in maintaining the freedom of the consciences of his Catholic subjects and, as therein necessarily involved, the freedom of the Spanish Church.

It seems, therefore, that in all cases, the end of the mediæval theocracy in Spain has come, and it only remains to be seen whether the rights of conscience and the freedom of the individual citizen will have to be gained through suffering under a democratic tyranny through parliamentary contests under a constitutional government, or, as is most unlikely, be allowed to grow and expand under the shelter of a sovereignty which might claim obedience from the most reactionary elements of Spanish society.

If we pass from the mountains where the more despotic form of what is presumed to be Spanish monarchy is struggling to assert itself, through southern France, to the Alps, we come to another nation which may seem to constitute the very political antipodes of Spanish monarchism, namely, Switzerland.

Yet in Switzerland we find a singular fundamental resemblance to Spain under a strangely different exterior.

The United States and Switzerland are republics, Spain and England monarchies. Thus are they classed in popular apprehension. Really, however (as most of my readers are doubtless aware), it is Switzerland and Old Spain, the United States and England, which ought to be classed together.

When, after the religious disruption of the sixteenth century, the Swiss Confederation settled down into a certain number of Catholic and a certain number of Protestant communities, an intimate union of Church and State became the rule in the respective cantons. The rigid theocracy of Geneva is well known to all, but in the Catholic as in the Protestant cantons, Church laws were enforced by secular authority, and thus much of mediæval theocracy has been preserved down to the present day by these small communities.

Now, however, repudiation of the Christian theocracy is making its way in Switzerland, but by a singular inversion it is the non-Christian part of the nation which is seeking to prolong its forms, while those who are *par excellence* the very representatives of that theocracy are being gradually driven to take up a position hostile to them. This inversion has arisen through changes by which, owing to the union of Church and State, power over the Church has come into the hands of those most hostile to her, and we have as a result the grotesque exhibition of ex-priests, who have violated all their own vows in the name of liberty of conscience, becoming the willing agents of an anti-Christian government in robbing and oppressing Christians amongst whom that government has enabled them to intrude.

In Berne we also find an anti-Christian government taking upon itself to decide what doctrines its fellow-citizens are to accept, to whose guidance they are to commit their consciences, and also to draw geographical boundary lines, on one or the other side of which citizens are or are not to be allowed to make use of each other's religious ministrations.

There can be little doubt but that this tyranny will in time so arouse consciences in opposition to it, that a separation between Church and State will have to be ultimately effected, and thus in Switzerland, as in France, England, and Spain, the Christian theocracy, on its old basis, will have ceased to exist.

Descending the Alps and Apennines to Brindisi, we traverse a country now undergoing changes peculiarly interesting in reference to our present inquiry, since there the Christian theocracy has its headquarters.

It may at first be thought singular that Italy, which was the *fons et origo* of the modern humanistic spirit, and which in physical science (as especially in anatomy and geology) was so far ahead of more northern nations, should have continued, from Turin to Naples, subject to a system of government which appeared so decidedly theocratic.

But, in fact, it was much less so than it seemed. Thus in Tuscany the revolution of 1869 caused a dukedom to disappear which nominally, indeed, supported Christianity, but which did so much more in the interest of the dukedom than of the Church. The profoundly antitheocratic Leopoldine laws were in full force, and now under Victor Emmanuel if there is no longer that State support for the Church which formerly existed, the impediments to its action have also disappeared.

To the popular mind of England the penultimate King of Naples was the very representative of priest-ridden monarchy. Really, however, though glad to make use of Church influence for the support of the throne, not many Catholic monarchs have been more anti-theocratic than the sovereign in question. Not only intolerant of the Jesuits, he would not even listen to Pope Pius, when as his guest at Gaeta he petitioned for a modicum of freedom for the Sicilian Church.

The destruction, then, of such systems of government in Italy was more the making apparent of what was before latent than any really considerable advance in the anti-theocratic direction. The advance had been made long before.

While the pope's civil princedom remained, and any community, even that of a single city, continued subject to his direct civil sway, the mediæval Christian theocracy might be said still to exist. With its disappearance, should it be final, disappears the logical basis of that system; then "Christendom" exists and can exist no longer, however some shreds and patches of it may for a time linger amidst the social phenomena of the succeeding period.

It is true that we see a curious and interesting example

of "survival" in the Russian Empire. There a very peculiar Christian theocracy still remains erect; perhaps in full force, and destined to further development. Signs, however, are not wanting that it is really a tottering structure, deeply undermined and honeycombed as it is by the efforts of religious dissidents. Nevertheless the future of Russia is a subject full of uncertainty, and a problem not less perplexing than abounding in interest, about which a word or two may be said later.

We now come to the last region which need occupy us in our brief survey of the leading features of the action of social political evolution on Christianity from the Middle Ages to the present day. This last region is Germany. Under existing circumstances it is the most interesting of all; for there before our eyes is being played out on a magnificent scale a remarkably involved struggle, in which mediæval and modern, Christian and pagan conceptions are entangling and disentangling themselves with singular complexity, and forming a labyrinth, the clue to which seems to have been strangely missed by most of the leaders of English public opinion.

Under the head of Germany must be included, not only the new German Empire under Prussia, but Austria also. Austria must be included on account of the important part played by Southern Germany in the national evolution from the thirteenth century to the present day.

In Germany the Christian theocracy attained in one

respect a development which it reached nowhere else; namely, in the number of its spiritual rulers who held direct civil sway,—the various prince-bishops and archbishops, such as those of Cologne, Mayence, Salzburg, etc., etc. Besides this, the kaisers had a certain sanctity of authority recognised by the ecclesiastical power beyond that of any other temporal ruler. According to the generally received opinion of the Middle Ages there was but one supreme temporal lord of Christendom — the emperor, as there was but one supreme spiritual lord —the pope; and it was in this widely diffused belief that the emperors in their struggles with the pontiffs found, perhaps, their main support.

With the weakening of the Christian theocracy waned also the power of the Holy Roman emperor, the independence of subordinate princes in Germany increasing, while elsewhere the central powers were strengthening themselves at the expense of the various subordinate local authorities.

The movement of the Reformation, the subsequent religious struggles, and the rise of Prussia, completed, as every one knows, the real destruction of the old system. Thus, when the Corsican despot finally put an end to that venerable imperial dignity, he really caused to disappear but the shadow of a shade. He little thought, however, of the Nemesis he was conjuring up, and how the chronic disease of Germany would be cured and its feebleness invigorated by the sharp cautery of his merciless invasions.

The old historic Christian German sovereignty, with its majestic hierarchical system, in the State as well as in the Church, in the early part of the Middle Ages, as powerful as it was magnificent, was indeed at an end; but with marvellous rapidity arose that strong instinct and sentiment of unity, of which we see the result to-day—a unity not based on Christianity (and now, indeed, in deadly contest with it), but reposing on race and nature only, and in perfect harmony with that reviving paganism which in the first chapter of this essay it was endeavoured to describe. Of this latent power Napoleon I.'s aggression elicited the manifestation, but the full force of it was reserved for the overthrow of Napoleon III. The course of evolution in Germany, then, has been substantially similar to that we have seen elsewhere out of Prussia, though so complex, that an exposition of the causes of local differences in its development would alone form a work of the highest interest. After the final religious effect of the Reformatory movement had subsided, the old imperial authority was, strange to say, amongst the first to evolve and develop the further growth of that spirit which was most fatal to its own foundation. The profoundly anti-Christian policy of Joseph II. anticipated that of the French revolution and of the pagan German government of to-day.

The spectre of sans-culottism at Paris frightened back the European sovereigns into a temporary reversal of previous action, and made them seek to revitalise the rapidly decaying mediæval theocracy in the selfish interest of their own power. The experiment has been short-lived; Austria has thoroughly changed her policy, and Christianity, whatever its future may be, seems likely to suffer but little from the incubus of so damaging a support. The equally selfish and essentially hypocritical system of Prussia has also ended, and given place to an antagonism capable of putting the vitality of German Christianity to the proof. Even then, by these two powers—Austria and Prussia,—which in different aspects may claim to be the nearest existing representatives of the old temporal head of Christendom, the Christian theocracy is finally disavowed. The northern kaiser has been ostentatiously welcomed in the old imperial city as the avowed author of a letter to the supreme head of that theocracy, in which the claims of that head are repudiated and his authority defied.

It is true that the southern emperor is the *crowned* king of Hungary, and that his present conduct seems only to have been forced on him by circumstances, after years of fruitless efforts to found his empire on some modification of the old theocratic basis, much of which, indeed, still remains within the bounds of his empire. His failure is but a still greater proof of the irresistible force of the adverse current he has in vain tried to stem.

It is true, again, the northern emperor is the *crowned* king of Prussia; he has repeatedly protested that his power has a divine sanction, and he has been ever personally opposed to the anti-Christian policy in which he is now engaged. His crown, however (like that of Napoleon I.), was placed upon his head by his own hand—an act in itself virtually amounting to repudiation of a Christian theocratic basis, while the actions of his government have rapidly become more and more profoundly anti-Christian.

To sum up, then, the results of our survey: it may be asserted that since the days of St. Louis one movement has in the main continued almost uninterruptedly, in spite of actions of an apparently conflicting tendency.

This process has been one of continuous disintegration of the mediæval Christian theocracy, proceeding with varying degrees of rapidity over the whole area of what was once Christendom.

This movement, since it first displayed itself, has been aided and accelerated, not only by processes manifestly in harmony with it, but also by others which were intended and seemed calculated to arrest, or even reverse it.

The whole current of events became turned in one direction, and whether here or there princely power was augmented or diminished, whether popular liberties were curtailed or increased, whether aristocracies arose or decayed, all has aided in diverse ways this, which seems to have been the great dominant movement from mediæval times to our own.

Every effort which has been made to stem the current has failed; every power which raised itself in opposition has been broken.

In vain the Pilgrimage of Grace, with its banner of the five holy wounds, strove in fair fight to maintain the established system; in vain the misguided efforts of the Powder Plot sought by nefarious measures to restore it; in vain the virtues and conscientious efforts of Mary of England tried to retain the English crown to the Church; in vain the winning graces of Mary of Scotland sought similarly to retain the Scotch. Priests bled at Tyburn, English and Irish citizens suffered confiscation, exile, and death, in fruitless efforts to reverse or to impede the anti-theocratic course of events. The very atmosphere which repelled the Armada favoured the Dutch invasion, and blood flowed unavailingly at Culloden and the Boyne. The efforts of the French league were as resultless (in their intended direction) as the infamous dragonnades of Louis XIV., or the heroism of La Vendée. The white cockade of the Restoration but intensified the anti-theocratic hatred of France; and the apparently strong bands imposed by the Holy Alliance and Treaty of

Vienna proved really but cobwebs to the expansive efforts of advancing paganism, while the last Napoleon, powerful in invoking it in Italy and Austria, proved utterly impotent in his efforts to exorcise the spirit he had raised. The loyal troops of Francis Joseph, though momentarily all but triumphing against both France and Prussia, nevertheless actually failed against both, and the success of Germany in the recent war, instead of confirming and extending over the whole empire that modified theocracy which existed so peacefully and prosperously in Prussia, has had a directly opposite result.

It would seem that an action so wide-spread, so continuous, and so deep, proceeding as it is with accelerated rapidity, cannot easily be arrested, but rather must continue to proceed much further.

Nevertheless, there are many who believe that a reversal will at length ensue, and some modification of the old theocracy be again generally established. At present the only power which seems to contain enough of the old material is Russia. It *may* be that, instead of politically assimilating itself to western Europe (like the manners of its highest class), it may come to exercise a powerfully reactionary tendency. It does not seem impossible that, availing itself of the mutually enfeebling wars and revolutionary disintegrations of western powers, it may hereafter come to play that part in Europe which was played of old by Macedon in Greece.

Such a western expansion might be greatly aided if, carrying out the idea of a former sovereign, it united itself to the Roman Church, and made itself the agent of the most powerful religious feelings and of all the theocratic reactionary tendencies latent in western Europe. It does not even seem impossible that a Roman pontiff effectively restored to his civil princedom by such Russian agency might inaugurate, by a papal consecration in the eternal city, yet a fresh dynasty of "Holy Roman emperors," a Sclavonic series succeeding to the suppressed German line, as the Germans succeeded in the person of Charlemagne to the first line of Cæsars.

Nevertheless, such a transformation would be so great a reversal of the course which history has now pursued for six hundred years, that it can only be regarded as a remotely possible solution of the problem offered to us by the peculiar social and political divergence of Russia from the rest of Europe.

Again: if the expectation of continued social evolution in the path now so long followed be disappointed, and if Christian theocracy, but slightly modified from what has before existed, be restored, Christianity *can* of course have nothing to fear from such a change from subordination to supremacy. We may here, therefore, neglect all possibilities of reaction in a theocratic direction, since the subject of our inquiry concerns the probable result of the continued progress of resurging paganism, on the hypothesis that it continues to follow the same course as heretofore.

It is difficult to believe but that further progress in the course hitherto pursued can mean anything else than the entire cessation of political support to Christianity, whether in schools, the legislature, the head of the State, or the formalities officially recognised as concerning the birth, sexual relations, or death of citizens. Each man will then be everywhere free without political penalties of any kind to live, marry, carry on all social relations, die, and be buried in open rejection of the Church and her agency if he be so minded; and no State recognition or favour will tend to bribe individuals to simulate the acceptance of a creed which in their hearts they reject.

What, then, must be the effect on the Christian Church of such a universal repudiation of the Christian theocracy? Clearly, if that Church be essentially bound up with society as it has existed since mediaeval times, such repudiation must be simply fatal.

It is not wonderful that so very many Christians view with alarm and dismay the progress of this great pagan movement. In the first place the Christian Church has intimately connected itself with the Christian State: in the liturgy of royal coronations; in the past sanction of and sympathy with aristocratic institutions; in the tradition to the secular arm; in the Christian origin of so many universities; in the congregations devoted to instruction, to the sick, the aged, and the poor, through the accepted intervention of the State ; in the general tendency of the altar to ally itself to the throne, as in the France of to-day, in Spain, and in Austria.

Secondly, the enemies of the theocracy are the avowed enemies of Christianity itself, as in Spain, as with the French red republicans, as in Austria and Germany, and as with the most free-spoken democrats here in England.

Thirdly, in the past the destruction of the theocracy has undeniably been often the precursor of the destruction of religion itself, by the expulsion of citizens who have taken religious vows, the sequestration of their property, the restraint of their persons, occasionally by their actual slaughter.

Fourthly, vast religious changes have so often been due to political passion, as in England and Germany in the sixteenth century, and in Germany now; while sometimes national prejudice, as in Prussia and the United States in the present day, acts powerfully to render minds hostile to particular creeds. These considerations may well cause Christians to dread the further advance of modern political change. But the question then arises, Is there any compensating and restorative action which, not being obvious, escapes the notice of these alarmists ?

It may be that the existing social fabric is but one of several or of many political modes, with each of which Christianity can co-exist, and that the disintegrating changes are harmless to it, since they will but occasion the evolution of a new power.

If we regard the Church as a complex organism, it must, like every other organism, live by a series of actions responsive to the effects produced on it by the environment.

The action of the environment may be either to disintegrate and destroy, or to consolidate and perfect it, and such action will destroy the Church if it is not able to effect internal modifications adequately responding to external changes.

It is manifest that a great process of *external disintegration* has taken place as regards the Church's social relations—a process crippling its power of action on its old basis. The question then is, Has this action been or not been accompanied by a process of *internal integration* which has more and more perfected and strengthened the Church's power of action on a new basis, and fitted it better than ever before for the struggles of the future?

To ascertain the probable efficacy of such integrating action, if it exists, we must first endeavour to find out what is the social system likely to replace that which seems to be passing away, and must pass away if the existing anti-theocratic movement continues to augment and develop itself. We must thus inquire, in order to see whether the integrations arising in the Christian Church are or are not calculated so to meet the effects of the disintegrations as to place the ecclesiastical organism of the future in harmony with its new environment. Every social fabric, every considerable aggregation of mankind, must since men are rational animals, repose upon some reasonable principles resolvable ultimately into one of two ideas, "expediency" or "right," or into some combination of them.

A community of savages may perhaps continue to exist on the simple principle that infringement of the accepted tribal customs is equivalent to a broken head or a spear in the thigh. But this is a form of expediency. More highly organized social states may be conceived, under certain circumstances, to indefinitely cohere from force of habit and a perception of utility essentially like the preceding. On the other hand, such a persistent condition may be largely indebted for its persistence to a respect for ancient custom which, if explicitly or implicitly enjoined on citizens, becomes essentially the acceptance of some such *moral* aphorism as, "It is proper to maintain ancient customs;" and "This is a form of right."

As soon, however, as civilization has in any community attained a considerable development, the question of the basis of the social fabric will be sure to address itself to an increasing number of its component units.

A highly complex social system like that of England to-day reposes partly on perceptions of utility, but far more on moral ideas of two kinds—one being that of a divine appointment, the other that of absolute right.

The idea of utility or expediency may frequently be much more prominent and obtrusive, both in explanation and precept, than the moral conceptions. But it would nevertheless be difficult to deny that a belief in "divine appointment" widely prevails, at least in our agricultural districts, and that the conception of "absolute right" is a considerable, if not a main agent, in the diffusion of democratic ideas among our artisans.

Though it is manifest that our social system is largely maintained through a belief that things "work well," yet much that is put down to "expediency" will, when fully analysed, be found really to repose on a "moral" basis. Thus, Mr. Mill's so-called "Utilitarianism," aiming, as it professes to do, at the greatest happiness of *all sentient beings*, is really a distorted and exaggerated form of "absolute morality."

It seems indeed, to say the least, very doubtful whether any social fabric could enduringly repose upon simple and naked expediency and real utilitarianism; that is, that the temporal welfare of the individual should be to him his only end, and that he should recognise no obligation on any citizen or section of a community to regard the welfare or desires of others in the smallest degree beyond what self-interest may dictate. The moment any one asserts that a citizen ought to restrain his actions within such bounds that they do not impede the purely self-regarding actions of his fellows, he steps beyond utilitarianism into the region of "absolute morality." All he can consistently urge is that *it is expedient for each man to seek to establish and maintain* a social system in which *all actions are free to every citizen which do not directly infringe the similar freedom of his fellows.* This may be asserted to be expedient, since thus alone can each man best secure the steady and least impeded exercise of his own volition.

But whether or not a social fabric could be maintained in which it could not be proclaimed that to disregard others is *wrong*, as well as *inexpedient*, certain is it that if maintained it might become the most fearful of tyrannies. In such a social system the extermination of a harmless minority could only be opposed on the ground that it might be prejudicial to the majority.

Turning then to the other idea, that of "Right," it is manifest that it may repose upon either of two bases.

(1) A *supernatural revelation*, if a belief in that revelation be all but universal in any given society.

(2) A common belief as to *natural absolute right*, if any sufficient ethical proposition can be found which will command the assent of the overwhelming majority.

Social systems based on an asserted divine revelation—*i.e.*, theocracies—have played a most important part in social evolution up to this day; and no theocracy has played so great a one as that, the disintegration of which we are engaged in considering.

It is evident that naked self-assertion is a relatively feeble base for a national theocracy, and that some objective testimony is requisite to sustain, for any prolonged period, the claim of any man or body of men to supernatural authority.

This testimony did exist in mediæval Christendom. The government of each nation could appeal to a venerated external witness, namely, to the Church, as existing in other nations, and to the supreme head of that Church, whose decisions were accepted as final. No such testimony exists for any of the competing systems which claim a divine authority to-day—such as that of the Russian czar or of the Prussian monarchy, as understood by its king. It is also difficult to conceive that any similar testimony can come to be made use of by any non-Christian theocracy hereafter to arise.

It would thus seem that the social systems of the future must come to repose merely upon natural and intuitive right, unless mankind should revert to some form of Christian theocracy.

But what basis of natural right can be devised which the different races will agree to regard as of unquestionable solidity?

Those who agree in affirming that man's intellect has a power of apprehending "right" and "wrong" as distinct from "pleasurable" and "painful," may for all that differ widely as to what are and what are not the dictates of conscience in matters of even little complication. Nevertheless, however great may be such divergence, there is one dictum which they will generally recognise as indisputable; viz., that *no citizen has the right to deny to another a liberty which he, as a citizen, claims for himself.*

This is the converse of that principle which we have seen may be based upon a utilitarian foundation, and it is essentially the same as the fundamental principle of social ethics enunciated by Mr. Herbert Spencer in his "Social Statics"—the right of each man to do all save that which limits the similar rights of others.

If Mr. Herbert Spencer had no other merit, deep gratitude and great honour would be due to him for having with such vigour and efficiency vindicated this fundamental principle of natural sociology.

The utilitarian maxim, when impregnated with the moral aphorism, becomes a sure ground whereon the rights of minorities and of the individual may repose. Without that aphorism, however, they have no security. The absolute distinction between the "right" and the "pleasurable" being denied, inconvenient minorities cease to have any shelter from the *absolute* dominion of the majority—a frightful doctrine long latent and now become apparent in modern "Liberalism."

Such sentiments are, strange to say, the logical outcome of that philosophical system favoured by the London University and so popular in this eminently free country—a system which denies all absolute truth and all distinctions of kind between "right" and "pleasure."

Such a system—the monistic philosophy—recognising no distinction of kind between God and nature, the natural and the supernatural, man and brute, the good and the pleasant, naturally and logically asserts the *absolute* right of the state to control all and everything in the life of every individual citizen, and necessarily denies all rights to individuals or minorities. In principle it warrants the performance of acts incomparably more atrocious than the massacre of St. Bartholomew or the burnings of the Spanish Inquisition.

The perpetrators of those crimes, however bloody their acts, never put forth *a theory* which denied *all rights* to their victims. But there is no principle on the view advocated by Professor Huxley's school to which a minority might appeal in bar of utter extermination by a majority, if unable to convince the majority that it would injure *itself* by that minority's destruction.

Such is the natural political development of the monistic philosophy. It was so in the old pagan days, and it is tending to reappear with the revival of paganism as was before asserted* in the first chapter of this essay.

---

* See p. 29.

But if a freer social system results merely from the addition of the idea of "absolute morality" to that of "expediency," all those who go yet farther and assert the existence of a personal God, whose essence is absolutely moral, have a yet securer and wider basis for freedom. All such must also assert that each man has a right freely to perform all such actions as God through his conscience has enjoined him to perform, provided they do not deprive other men of similar freedom to fulfil what they believe to be their duty.

Thus the greatest amount of personal freedom comes to rest on a basis of "divine right," since, in the absence or non-recognition of a divine revelation limiting its exercise, such personal freedom becomes God-given and absolute.

Similarly all who hold such belief must assert that all the citizens of a state combined together save *one*, are morally incompetent by their joint authority as citizens to compel that *one* to perform an act against his conscience such as would be an outward act of adoration to a Deity in whom he disbelieved, or of insult to Him whom he conceives to be his Creator and his Lord.

Similarly they must allow that if two citizens agree in believing that one of them has a God-given jurisdiction over the other, the one must be free to yield voluntary obedience to the other in all that does not affect the equal rights of other citizens.

They must also admit that those citizens who agree in holding similar views as to their relations to God must be free to exert such combined actions as do not interfere with the analogous rights of combination of other citizens.

Again, they cannot logically deny to citizens freedom to declare their belief to those who ask them, and especially to teach their children themselves or to select other citizens to whom they may choose to delegate that office.

CHAPTER III.

THREE IDEALS.

THERE are thus, as we have seen, now struggling for supremacy THREE DISTINCT IDEALS, three distinct socio-political systems, and two are mixed up and blended in the great movement which has been described as reviving paganism.

That great modern movement has been and is so powerful because it is invigorated by the temporary union of these two essentially divergent and conflicting tendencies of ideals.

(1.) The first of these is the mainly unconscious and partly conscious real pagan revival and revolt against God,—PAGANISM.

(2.) The other is the spirit of freedom, the assertion of natural right, and revolt against the domination of man (*merely as man*) over his fellow,—CIVICISM.

Besides these there is also that with which the pagan revival has conflicted and conflicts, namely :—

(3.) The tendency to preserve, or more or less bring back, the mediæval Christian theocracy,—MEDIÆVALISM.

These three tendencies are actually mixed up in the most complex manner in modern, social, and political struggles, as we shall shortly see.

The efforts of those who strive for the third ideal need not here occupy us, since our subject is the action upon Christianity of the modern movement—on the supposition that it continues.

The first tendency, that towards true conscious paganism, may indeed, as was said in the first part of this essay, present us with some startling developments in the future.

Nevertheless, when once completely dissociated from the spirit of civicism, its force must greatly diminish, and if the re-appearance of a Spanish grand inquisitor in the flesh is about as likely as that of a plesiosaurus, a general enduring return to the old paganism must be still more unlikely, though the spread of pantheism at the present time is portentous.

There is then reason to believe that the second tendency and ideal, that of freedom reposing both upon expediency and absolute God-given right is the consummation towards which society is, on the whole and in general, tending, widely divergent as may be really or apparently its direction here and there.

In England, its colonies, this tendency is now triumphant. The same may still be said of the United States, though greed of power on the part of an unscrupulous president now threatens to stir up religious strife by a wanton invasion of religious equality. Few sights could be more grievous and depressing than would be that of a great nation led into a reactionary policy of religious oppression in the miserable interest of a "third term," or even the spectacle of a large number of citizens of a really free country persuaded to barter liberty and conscience for the indulgence of sectarian animosity by legislation directly counter to the whole process of social evolution, as displayed in the history of the last six centuries. Such a course of conduct would be the more deplorable, seeing that the United States have reaped the advantage of that evolutionary process without having had to uproot or destroy systems previously established; so that the throwing away of the advantages they have so peacefully gained would be a peculiarly gratuitous and wanton act. The example of England, however, is telling powerfully upon other nations, and happily the rapidity with which the English-speaking races are multiplying will tell yet more, since in a few centuries "English" will be *the* language of the world.

Nevertheless the action of the first (pagan or monistic) tendency is to be feared as a powerful agent hostile to freedom, existing concealed amongst those who are now active in the destruction of the last relics of the mediæval theocracy in the name of liberty. Such agents are seeking to destroy them, not in the interest of natural freedom, but for the establishment of a revived paganism and dominant and intolerant "naturalism" to which they are passionately attached. They therefore seek to bind in fetters the opponents of their unchristian *anti-theocracy*, the establishment and endowment of which they desire to effect. Hence those justifications and laudations of active persecution to which Professor Huxley and others* have given utterance.

Our empire, by a happy combination of circumstances, and by the merits of the races which inhabit it, has long been the conspicuous assertor of freedom. The sentiment in favour of wide liberty to the individual citizen—in speech, in writing, in locomotion and association—has not only taken deep hold of our own people, but also of the population of that magnificent transatlantic republic, the greatest glory of which is the perfect freedom of its citizens.

By a series of happily devised measures perseveringly perfected through more than a century, this civic liberty has been defined and ever more efficiently guarded,—the tyrannical measures of Stuart as of Tudor being repudiated in principle no less than practically.

It is to be hoped that the force of this traditional current in favour of individual liberty in England is too strong to be reversed or turned aside. Nevertheless there is a certain danger that the "No Popery" prejudice may

---

* *E.g.*, "In the judgment of history the *tyrannisms of free thought* may be justified."—*Westminster Review*, October, 1873, p. 413. On this subject see "Lessons from Nature" (Murray, 1876), chapter xiii., p. 396.

to such an extent favour the efforts of the anti-Christian fanatics as to prejudice the conservatism of our civic freedom.

At the least it has influenced public opinion with regard to continental politics, so far that the leaders of that opinion condone or even applaud measures which are directly opposed to all our traditional Liberal legislation.

This no doubt is partly owing to the complexity of the struggle going on between Church and State in Germany, and a failure to distinguish between two very different sets of actions which are respectively the expression of the two different tendencies which have been above distinguished as civicism and paganism.

One of these, civicism, is the continuance of the general movement hostile to Christian theocracy, the tendency of which movement is to break off religion from connection with the State, and to withdraw from those citizens who choose to devote themselves to religion all exceptional privileges, and all power or control over the civil acts of those who do not voluntarily seek their ministry. With this movement the traditional Liberals of England may well enough sympathise.

The other—the pagan, or monistic—tendency, is to convey to the numerical majority of the nation an absolute power over all the external manifestations of internal belief, an absolute power over their persons and their property; in a word, to erect a more thorough and degrading despotism than Europe has seen since the downfall of the pagan Cæsars.

No doubt many honest men favour the Prussian Church Laws because they see that they favour the first tendency, and because they do not perceive how they are really inspired by the second or pagan spirit.

This confusion is favoured by those who (however justly they may assert their legal or their treaty rights) oppose the laws by protests in favour of the "liberty of the Church," "Christian marriage," the "rights of the bishops," etc. An opposition necessarily futile (unless the whole modern movement can be reversed or arrested), because "civicism" knows nothing of "the Church," or "Christianity," or "bishops," as such (only recognising individual citizens and their rights against reciprocal encroachment), while "paganism" hates all three.

On the other hand, many of those who advocate the new laws out of a spirit of opposition to mediævalism, forget, or do not understand, that they are trampling on the most fundamental rights of their fellow-citizens, and erecting a tyranny which has much less to say in its defence, and is indefinitely more autocratic in its principles than the old system they, in the spirit of their age, oppose.

According to the spirit of modern freedom, individuals are perfectly free — with the limitations before mentioned — to form themselves into associations in which their mutual relations are regulated by mutual consent, and free to exclude from their voluntary society individuals who do not conform to the rules they have freely chosen for their own regulation;—no one citizen having the right to intrude himself upon the society of others who do not approve of him.

But the new laws, in fact, deny to citizens the right to group and associate themselves in voluntary associations, to select freely from their fellow-citizens those to whom they will confide the education of their children, or to obey the dictates of their conscience by acts which are innocent of encroaching on the similar rights of other citizens.

To deny the right of an episcopally nominated Roman Catholic priest to officiate in a parish, the Roman Catholic parishioners of which desire him, is to infringe, not so much his rights, as the rights of election of those citizens who by the fact that they call themselves Roman Catholics show that they have delegated that power to their bishop, and that they elect as their minister that citizen who is selected by such bishop. To exile or imprison such Roman Catholic bishop is to outrage the rights of a yet greater number—the Roman Catholics of the diocese, who show by their calling themselves *Roman* Catholics that they, in fact, voluntarily elect as the citizen to whom they will stand in a certain voluntary relation—that one who is indicated to them by, and who is in communion with the Roman pontiff.

To attempt to impede excommunication, is to deny to citizens the right to exclude from a voluntary society members who do not conform to freely chosen rules.

To violate the freedom of person and property of citizens without trial, without even one distinct definite accusation—even though such citizens call themselves Jesuits—is a glaring injustice; but greater, though less glaring, is the tyranny thereby inflicted on thousands of citizens whose rights of choice and election are violated by such acts, and whose most earnest desires and wishes as to themselves, and their children and friends, are thereby trampled on.

The citizens calling themselves Jesuits have gross wrong done them; their parents, brothers, sisters, and personal friends suffer hardships hardly less patent; but unnoticed and apparently unthought of are the wrongs of the thousands who have been deprived of their greatest comfort — thousands of the most innocent and most helpless citizens of the State. Who can tell the hundreds of fond mothers, faithful wives, and tender sisters who have bitterly wept the forced departure of the guardians and supporters in virtue of wayward sons, errant husbands, and erring brothers. These and cognate considerations will reveal a mass of silent suffering, suffering perhaps greater than that produced by many a bloody battlefield.

The effect of bias, so strongly put forward by Mr.

Herbert Spencer in the "Study of Sociology" could hardly find a better exemplification than the dispositions felt by so many Englishmen to these acts. This may be made clear if we suppose similar acts under other circumstances. Let us suppose that a law was passed that no one might assume, or change, an office in any Freemasons' lodge without the expressed assent of the Government; also, that no member of the Freemasons' body, whatever secrets he might have violated or rules transgressed, might be officially blamed in or be excluded from masonic society without the permission of the Government being first asked and obtained. It is hardly likely but that even non-masonic Englishmen would deem such legislation a daring infringement of the liberties of the subject.

But if another law were passed summarily expelling from England all Freemasons and confiscating Masonic property, what would be the outcry! This, however, is by no means all. We must further suppose, that a law was passed giving the police authorities power at their discretion, to declare, without proof, any man or woman whatever, belonging to any voluntary association, to be, in spite of their denials, affiliated masons, and to expel them accordingly. The iniquity of the measure is so monstrous as to impair the force of the supposition by its very monstrosity, and the impossibility of really conceiving it to be done in England.

Yet this is literally what has taken place in Prussia with the applause, *mirabile dictu*, of "LIBERALS." It is of the A, B, C of our system, that no man should be punished without a trial. Yet in Germany, because citizens happen voluntarily to belong to a private society which has not a fragment of power over its members beyond what such members voluntarily concede—nay, even because police authorities choose, without evidence produced, to *say* that any citizens are affiliated to such a society—they have, not only been held up to public ignominy by official utterances, but have actually been torn away from friends and relations and their locomotion restricted within narrow limits, or they have been expelled the country, and their very persons, in some instances, treated with cruel violence.

These citizens are meantime accused of no definite crime; in spite of demands, they are brought to no trial and have no opportunity given them of self-justification.

As we said just now, the effect of bias could hardly go further than to make Englishmen, who blame the expulsion of the Moors and Jews from Spain, applaud such acts.

And what is the authority that dares thus to outrage and trample on the primary rights of citizens? The German government is a modern one; it is based on the modern basis—popular will, not on an asserted and externally recognised God-given power like that of the thrice-crowned kaisers of mediæval times.

It is true that the emperor in his not very wise and not very truthful * letter to the pope, talks about his "responsibility to God" for his sovereign acts, and it is generally supposed he asserts for himself a divine right. But for this assertion he has nothing to show, no external witness, as before said, or objective testimony. If Kaiser Wilhelm can raise the dead, he may resuscitate in his Berlin subjects a belief in his own supernatural authority. But the acts of his Government lead more and more in the anti-theocratic direction, and its true basis will thus be more and more plainly avowed to be the will and consent of the majority of his subjects. It comes then

---

* "Not very wise," because his reply as to what Protestants believe concerning "One Mediator," has nothing whatever to do with the pope's remark respecting the necessary consequences of baptism. "Not very truthful," for two reasons: first, because he therein implies an accusation of treason against citizens who in vain ask for an opportunity of showing their innocence by a public trial, the laws of Prussia not enabling the bishops to BRING AN ACTION FOR LIBEL AGAINST THE MINISTER by whom the letter is countersigned; secondly, because he replies to what every one knows was not the pope's meaning. The pope, of course, knew well enough that according to constitutional fictions, *the emperor* must *officially* approve of all his minister's acts, but La Marmora's book has shown us how in the past he was led by his minister in opposition to his real private wishes. The pope, of course, hoped and thought that in the recent Church laws he was also being led in opposition to his private wishes, and some who know the Berlin court well still believe that in so thinking the pope was right.

to this, that the actual or apparent majority of Germans claim the power to dispose absolutely and without appeal of the minority; to dictate to them their mutual voluntary relations, determine the amount of their locomotion, or even their very residence within the land—to fix for them the dogmas of their creed and their mode of worship, and to enforce the education of their children in a belief directly contradicting that of their parents.

Yet the *Times* has gone the length of asserting that Prussia has the right to do this now, because of what we did three hundred years ago in England, as if no progress had taken place within that period, even were the circumstances the same, which they manifestly are not.

Yet the *Times* would hardly venture to approve of the passing of a "bill of attainder" against a political opponent of the English sovereign of to-day, or the summary decapitation of any illustrious lady whose existence might be personally inconvenient to some future chief ruler.

But the circumstances are manifestly not the same. They are not so, because the bishops and clergy generally may, in the absence of conspicuous protests to the contrary, be fairly taken as the representative of the religious opinions of those to whom they minister. Now in England the great majority of the clergy submitted to the change which Henry VIII. introduced. The act of his legislature which abolished State recognition of papal supremacy in England did not violate the rights of citizens in anything like the degree in which the recently made Church laws of Germany violate them. Again, the English Church of the sixteenth century was that of the entire people; but in Prussia the persecuted Church is that of but a portion, and its legal rights and the claims of its members on the State are different in different regions, according to the date and the terms of the acquisition of such regions by the Prussian kings. There is yet another contrast in our favour. What we did we did openly and above-board, but the German Government has by its agents added the meanness of mendacity to brutal outrage; since it has now and again been asserted that the Roman Catholic religion is not persecuted, and while papal supremacy is not in express terms abolished, it is virtually and effectively set aside and practically annulled. A new State religion is, in fact, set up and sought to be forced upon citizens by the May laws. To ask Roman Catholic citizens to acquiesce in such laws is to ask them to lie—to apostatise from their religion, and at the same time to pretend to adhere to it. In *principle* there is no difference whatever between asking a Roman Catholic of to-day to perform some outward act of assent to the recent Church legislation of Germany and asking a primitive Christian to burn incense to the genius of the emperor.

A demand on Roman Catholics to admit that Dr. Reinkens is a Catholic bishop is a grotesque insult to their reason as well as an outrage to their conscience.* It amounts to a demand that they should recognise the majority of their fellow-citizens as having the power to determine for them what they shall deem to be essential characters of their own spiritual chiefs. On this principle the emperor's government might require that the title of "Catholic bishop" should be given to Baron Rothschild, and hardly less absurd would be the requisition that Bismarck should be everywhere in Germany received and treated as a "*princess.*"

It is a matter of deep regret that religious antipathy should cause many in England to sympathise with acts so entirely opposed to English social and political principles, but the outcome will probably bring about a juster view.

---

* The complete abandonment of the Christian standpoint by those who advocate new State religions, even when such advocates are disguised as ecclesiastics, is curiously illustrated by the declaration of Dr. Reinkens (when taking his oath to the State). He then declared that if the State should hereafter require of him acts inconsistent with his duty as a Christian bishop, *he would resign his office* rather than oppose it. Now the universally received ideal of a Christian bishop is that of a shepherd who feeds his flock with sound doctrine and protects it from the attacks of mundane wolves. What Dr. Reinkens asserts as incumbent upon him he, of course, by implication asserts to be also the duty of other bishops. Thus, according to him, the duty of bishops in the presence of a Government which has become hostile to Christianity is to *desert their charges* and to leave their starving flocks to the mercy of the wolves, as this eminent pastor professes beforehand his readiness to do: "The hireling fleeth, because he is an hireling, and careth not for the sheep."

That such acts should be applauded by many and tolerated by more in Germany is not surprising, for two reasons: first, because of the grinding tyranny under which that country has so long lain, it is not wonderful that freedom is not really prized when it is not experimentally known. It is not surprising, secondly, because of the prodigious extent to which Hegelianism, or some cognate form of pantheism, has filtered down through society in all directions. Hence, a willing idolatry of "the State" as of some all potent fetish. It seems hardly to occur to any one, then, to ask the single question, "What is the State?" and to recognise the truth that this much venerated "State" is but a name for the governing majority of the citizens. When this simple fact becomes generally known, the sacred right of any score of men to regulate the actions, words, and thoughts of any dozen, will in all probability cease to be acquiesced in with so much reverential and unquestioning awe, and citizens will be less ready to prostrate themselves before the car of such a Juggernath as the military despotism which calls itself "the State" in Prussia.

Fortunately, however, in such action as is now going on in Prussia and Switzerland, an effect is being produced exactly contrary to that which the actors desire.

That such a contrary effect should be produced is quite in accordance with Mr. Herbert Spencer's whole teaching. He tells us: "Feelings called into play . . . will strengthen, while those which have diminished demands on them will dwindle."*

Under the sway of a benevolent government there is a certain natural tendency amongst Christians to feeble volitions in support of their religion, from the small opportunities offered for the energetic exercise of such volitions. On the other hand, a persecution such as is now going on tends, as so many of the elections prove (more even by the increase in the number of opposition voters than by the number of Christian members returned), to elicit acts which by their very exercise strengthen the feelings and stimulate the volitions which gave them birth. Moreover, as the persecution increases in intensity, the reaction in favour of civic freedom (already evinced by no inconsiderable support) will also increase, and these effects must continue till the cause is removed. More and more respect and sympathy for the Roman Catholic clergy will be felt and manifested by an increasing number of Protestants who see that the former are fighting their battle also, and who admire their courage and constancy. Thus a great strengthening of the Roman Catholic Church in Prussia cannot but be the final result of these hostile efforts, since the times do not admit, as yet, of a bloody war of extermination.

Nevertheless, the anti-theocratic tendency will probably remain too powerful to allow of a simple reversal of the

---

* " Study of Sociology," p. 372.

recent legislation, and thus a *tertium quid* will be arrived at by the consent of the Roman Catholics, and of those who, being in favour of civic freedom, do not (like the Reinkenists and fanatical pagans) desire the State establishment of a rival system.

This *tertium quid* must be the severance of Church and State—another important step in that great process of six centuries' growth which it has been here endeavoured to depict.

To return from this digression: it seems that social evolution, if it continues to advance along the same path as hitherto, must mean the entire destruction of the mediæval Christian theocracy.

If this destruction should be accompanied by the universal enforcement of a rival pagan system, an *anti*-theocratic establishment, the effect would no doubt be most disastrous for Christianity. It may, however, be confidently affirmed that, whatever be the extravagances of the paganism to come, no attempt to erect a universal pagan *anti*-theocratic and pantheistic despotism could resist the hostile coalition of Christians with all those who desire the natural liberty of the individual citizen. The monstrous claim of men, *as mere men*, to control and direct the consciences of their fellows, could never succeed in justifying itself to the human reason.

With a *régime* of true freedom, that is, where there is liberty and order, experience shows us that Christianity can grow and thrive.

If, instead of paganism, civicism gains the day (the second of the three systems now struggling for sway), it is difficult to see how the latter can have any positive religious effect whatever. The merely negative action of depriving all religions of any State support is but the forming of "a fair field and no favour," where success must depend on quite other than political causes.

Such, at least, is the conclusion which seems forced on us at a first glance, but a satisfactory conclusion cannot be arrived at without some further examination.

There are, however, not a few persons who apprehend that instead of our soon seeing an orderly system of civic freedom, European society is simply tending to disintegration and anarchy. Now, of course, a lapse into utter barbarism would necessarily carry with it a destruction of Christianity, since Christianity supposes the existence of a certain degree of natural social evolution; such, *e.g.*, as that of "the family"—an institution at which the hostile efforts of the most "advanced" reformers are directly aimed.

It is certainly conceivable that at least such anarchy as lately arose in parts of Spain, and as prevailed for a short time in Paris, might extend itself over a much wider area. Not many of those who enjoyed the most refined *salons* of the French capital under Louis XV. would have believed it possible that all France before the century ended could have presented the spectacle that it did during the worst moments of the "Terror." Men may have similar blindness to-day.

We have seen how that support of our European social organisation, which consisted in a widely diffused belief in its divine ordination, has been gradually withdrawn, and naturally and necessarily the support derived from a simple acceptance of Christian morality is concomitantly weakened—that morality being replaced by other systems, and ultimately by the teaching which now issues from our nationally supreme sources of culture. (1) That right is but another name for pleasure; (2) that temporal good is the only good to be sought after or desired; and (3) that no man has control over or is responsible for his actions.

It is difficult to think that the wide reception of these doctrines amongst the lowest classes will not be attended with very considerable transformations, and those are certainly not altogether devoid of rational grounds of apprehension, who fear that as the Græco-Roman civilisation was ruined through the invasion of barbarians from without, so existing civilisation may be destroyed through an eruption of barbarians from below. And when we consider the intimate relations existing between that civilisation and Christianity, there can be little cause for wonder either that Christianity itself should for a time share in such unpopularity as our social system may have acquired, or that that system itself should vanish simultaneously with a wide-spread, avowed, and open renunciation of the religion which gave birth to, and was so intimately blended with it.

Can Christian monarchy rationally survive for many centuries the dethronement of the power that consecrated it? Nobles, the descendants of those who robbed the Church—that is, the whole of their poorer fellow-citizens —for their own selfish aggrandisement, should hardly be surprised if fresh injustice again plunders them. A plutocracy of merchants, manufacturers, and wealthy professional men offers little to impress the masses with a sense of its inviolable sanctity.

The highest triumphs of art, magnificent decorations, the richest products of the loom, profusion of gold and jewels,—these things as used by the Church were at least for the enjoyment of the multitude. There will be little cause for astonishment if that multitude ultimately objects to the withdrawal of these things into the palaces of kings and of princes, whether feudal or mercantile; or to the exclusive appropriation of some of them for the private use of rich women, however virtuous, or of beauties however vile.

Wrong has been destroyed to give way to other wrong, injustice has been displaced by fresh injustice, till much honest indignation reinforces that spirit of revolt against our existing social system which so widely pervades the masses in the great European cities, producing an accumulated aversion from a civilisation which has cast off almost all the grace, with much of the material, and still more of the moral alleviations, which attended the earlier condition of the Christian theocracy.

It would be unjust to our species to deny the mitigating circumstances attending the surging of democratic passion to-day. Careworn toilers may view with complacency the glittering splendour of barons whose rank they view as God-ordained and yet evanescent, they being essentially and for eternity but the equals of themselves, whose humble path is no less God-appointed, and on that account no less worthy of esteem—both being actors for a little time upon the same stage, and to be judged not by their accidental trappings, but by their due fulfilment of their respective parts!

But this belief has been, and is being sedulously destroyed. Can we wonder that with its disappearance the same phenomena come to be viewed in a very different aspect?

Nevertheless, there are grounds for thinking that the violences of social antagonisms are on the whole likely to diminish, however noisily or brutally they may upon occasions here and there assert themselves. Even if Europe should become the scene of disorder which some fear, it is impossible that the whole world can simultaneously be the theatre of the most extreme and bloody red-revolutionary tyranny.

Those imbued with the doctrine of evolution can hardly accept a belief that the process of social development has culminated in Europe, considering how distant from attainable perfection is the stage already reached; and the assertion that it has done so in the whole world would probably be considered by them a manifest absurdity.

Going then to the extreme of what can be deemed possible, however wildly improbable, let us imagine that private freehold property in land has been universally abolished, that complicated regulations are in force tending everywhere to depress the capitalist at the expense of the artisan, that throughout Europe a persecution has raged which has resulted in the slaughter of every bishop and the majority of the clergy, as well as the abolition of every religious order, and the destruction of every single church. Let us suppose, also, that purely secular instruction is everywhere compulsorily given, and that relations between the sexes of the extremest degree of laxity become recognised by law. What would be the effect of so profound and extensive a revolution on the Christian Church? In the first place, the universality of that Church would manifestly enable its supreme head ever to find a shelter, and in the supposed condition of Europe that refuge might well be found in the great republic of the west. Similarly, institutions for the carrying on of the traditional culture of the clergy would for a time become extra-European.

The Church has no absolute necessity for property in land, as past persecutions have abundantly demonstrated.

The slaughter of bishops would but lead to the consecration of others desirous of shedding their blood for the faith, while the monarchal constitution of the Church, made still more marked since the Vatican Council, would enable the government of the European missionary Church to be carried on, if needful, without bishops, under the direct episcopal jurisdiction of the pope. The Church of Japan has survived through the rage of persecution without the aid even of a single priest, native or foreign.

The elevation of the artisan class, when once effected, would put an end to their hostility to the Church, since that hostility has mainly arisen from a belief that the action of the Church was prejudicial to their elevation. No inevitable antagonism divides the clergy as such from the humblest classes, and the illustrious head of the English Church has publicly shown in his own person how warm are His Eminence's sympathies for the depressed agricultural labourer.

Unless, again, we hereafter find reason to think that scientific and philosophical evolution will be fatal to the Church, the action of compulsory secular instruction *must* also ultimately result in such disappointment, since Christians would be forced once more, as of old, to give at home that intelligent and emotional training in doctrine and practice, the effect of which no public teaching can rival, and by which the influence of pagan schools was successfully combated in former times.

With the revoluntary changes here supposed once introduced, all the causes of the present popular antipathy to Christianity would be removed, except those resulting from fear of the attractive influences of its morality, and from the possible prevalence of an anti-Christian philosophy, the action of which will be considered in the next chapter.

The disorders springing from a general relaxation of sexual morality can hardly fail to give rise to a reaction in favour of Christian ethics on the part of an increasing portion of the population, if only through the gradual extinction by natural decay of the families of the most sexually vicious.

The abolition of religious orders must cease when once individual liberty for citizens begins to assert itself, since citizens cannot be free if they are not permitted by their fellow-citizens to live peaceably together in voluntary associations, eating, dressing, and reading according to their pleasure, as long as they limit not the similar rights of others.

But even before the introduction of such common individual freedom, it is almost impossible for the most tyrannical State to interfere with the practice of the evangelical counsels—voluntary poverty, chastity, and obedience. Each successive great epoch of the Church has been fruitful of fresh modes of their manifestation, and some new embodiment of the ascetic spirit has appeared for a time on the crest of the advancing wave of Christian aggression on the world. After the martyrs came the Fathers of the Desert, then the Benedictines, to be succeeded by the white-robed Cistercians, themselves to give way to the friars, whose influence was afterwards overshadowed by the valiant soldiers of Loyola. Arguing simply from analogy, it is not likely but that the same cause may produce again effects similarly appropriate to time and place. The old religious orders did not adopt picturesque or fantastic costumes, but slight modifications of fashions in vogue in their day amongst the poorest class, so that each at its origin appeared far less peculiar than at present.

Hard work and charity under one form or another were universally obligatory, and to this day the Trappist works like a day-labourer. It may well be then that manual toil in other forms, and a fresh modification of fraternal charity, will cause religious congregations to be as heartily welcomed and beloved by a socially democratic republican community as ever they were in the ninth, thirteenth, or sixteenth centuries.

Even under a communistic *régime*, presided over by some "Albert ouvrier," a body of workmen who were only distinguished from their fellows by a larger spirit of fraternity, and a disposition to take a greater share of work than others, while at the same time they appropriated a less portion of its fruit, would speedily be popular; and a love for God might soon come to be pardoned, when it was seen to be accompanied by an earnest and self-sacrificing love for man.

Sisters of Charity have met with respect even from the roughest of French "Reds," and all hostility to them would disappear when they ceased to be ideally connected with a political system which kept democracy in check, or sought so to keep it.

It, seems, then, that no necessarily fatal result to Christianity may be expected from the wildest political changes; but rather that an extreme advance of the modern spirit may give rise to fresh Christian developments. But such disorders as are here spoken of, such rapid and sudden destruction of the existing European social fabric, are really in the highest degree unlikely. It seems far more probable that a system of freedom on the English and American models, more and more approximating to what has been called civicism—that is, the ideal of Mr. Herbert Spencer—will be gradually, and in the majority of cases peacefully attained, although with much vexatious, though not violent, persecution from devotees of paganism. (See note, p. 122.) Should such be the real future, experience already shows us how disappointed will be those who expect the destruction of Christianity from political changes favourable to democracy.

In America we see before us undeniable evidence that the Church can not only exist, but grow and thrive, in the freest political atmosphere—shown more by the multiplication and spread of religious orders and the up-growth of a native-born clergy, than even by the augmentation of the episcopate. There (in New York) has arisen a new religious congregation—the Paulists—the founder and head of which, Father Hecker, is a typical example of the Church of the United States; not less conspicuous for love of his country and admiration of its politico-social system than for unhesitating and unquestioning obedience and loyalty to the head of his Church.

The United States have also supplied us with a crucial test of the power of the Church to resist the strongest secular influences hostile to its integrity.

During the late memorable war almost every uncatholic form of Christianity became split and divided into a northern and a southern, an anti-slavery and a pro-slavery body. The Church alone maintained its unity perfectly unbroken, and was thus enabled more efficiently to aid in healing the moral disunion, and allaying the heartburnings which remained after the victory, by which unbroken unity many earnest minds in the great republic have been deeply impressed.

In Belgium, again, we see how the Church can not only prosper under free institutions, but have so energetic and vigorous a life as to provoke a violent, though groundless dread of the re-establishment of mediævalism. How it lives in England and Ireland we see.

Again: the fact that complete civic freedom favours the Church's growth may be gathered from those who clamour for a retention of the last remnants of the old theocratic system as barriers to "ultramontanism." It is on this very ground that the separation between Church and State in Bavaria and South Germany is opposed by "Liberal Catholics," and that such a union is sought by Dr. Reinkens, while M. Loyson has proclaimed it an *honour* to Christianity to obtain State recognition and support. Even in England the disestablishment of the Anglican Church is opposed by those who dread the growth of definite "dogma" and "ecclesiastical tyranny," and clamour for "spiritual freedom," as understood by Dean Stanley and his school.

It seems, then, that the completion of the great modern anti-theocratic movement (if developed in the direction, not of a State-supported paganism, but in that of civicism —that system of mutual respect and individual freedom which expedience and natural morality agree to justify), by no means necessarily implies a weakening, still less a destruction of the Church; whilst facts are not wanting which seem to indicate a thence resulting increase in its vigour and efficiency. It is not sluggish majorities, but active, concentrated, and aggressive minorities which influence the world's course most effectually.

But a process of internal integration has been spoken of as possibly accompanying the external disintegration of that great complex organism, the Church. To make this manifest would require little less than a history of the development of Church doctrine and discipline from the thirteenth century to the present day. It will, however, hardly be contested that the whole course of such development has tended to give more and more precision and distinctness to the Church's dogmas, and efficiency to the action of its governing power. If the number of regular clergy has relatively diminished, the whole mass of the secular clergy (as it is often reproachfully said) has become more and more approximated to a great body of regulars. The perfection of the Church's organisation, the definiteness and clearness of doctrine it has attained, could not well have been made more manifest than by the acquiescence of the whole episcopate, without one solitary dissentient voice, in the recent Vatican Decrees. Thus, it cannot be denied that, *pari passu* with the disintegration arising from the increasing disability or disinclination of kings (or other and subordinate social authorities) to enforce the decisions and behests of the Church, the Church herself has simultaneously developed, by a process of integration, a vastly increased power of herself, promulgating, applying, and giving effect to them over all those who voluntarily accept her spiritual sway. The downfall of the chief pontiff's spiritual princedom, which marks the formal end of Christendom, was almost immediately preceded by the culmination of his spiritual power through the universal acceptance by the whole Church of his official infallibility, than which no step could be more calculated to give vigour, precision, and unanimity to the action of the whole body.

Moreover, even material inventions and improvements have strikingly co-operated in the same direction. The facilities afforded to locomotion, and the transmission of intelligence by railways and the electric telegraph, set at defiance the old restrictions as to the publication of bulls and other machinery of Church government.

It is also undeniable that outside the Church's organisation there has gone on a movement, parallel with the latter phases of the movement distinctive of the Christian theocracy. In England, besides the great tractarian and ritualistic development of Anglicanism, a movement towards increased orthodoxy or towards ecclesiasticism (*e.g.*, as evidenced architecturally), has gone on even in nonconformist bodies. In Germany, while on the one hand rationalism is increasing, on the other an upward reaction is setting in amongst evangelical Christians which the Bismarckian persecution cannot but aid in developing. Even in Holland there has been, and is,* a powerful and extensive movement in an upward direction.

---

* See *Contemporary Review*, November, 1873, p. 955.

Moreover, one important effect of the great modern movement will be to let in upon the Christian Church the full action of the destructive agencies of nature, commonly termed collectively "natural selection."

During the period in which the Church had full temporal support and sheltered within its fold whole nations, with hardly an avowed dissentient, the following merely natural effects must have inclined to mar its efficiency :—

1. Want of the stimulus of opposition, tending to diminish the vigour of efforts for its support and extension.

2. A similarly diminished need for the diffusion of a keen, intelligent, and reasoned apprehension of its doctrines and teachings.

3. A lowered moral tone from the influence of the indifferent majority—resulting in diminished efforts after a life in accordance with Christian precepts and counsels. This is owing to a diffusion over the whole body of the spirit governing the majority, which spirit in almost every large community is otiose and indifferent. In the days of the Church's temporal prosperity the indifferent were included within the Church, instead of being visibly external to it, and so tended to lower the tone of the whole.

Thus an unenergetic, tepid, unintelligently apprehensive, and morally inconsistent spirit, may but too naturally tend to diffuse itself over a temporally-supported, honoured and wealthy Church, which has no declared dissidents in the area in which it exists.

When such a theocratically organised Christian community becomes, by revolution, exposed to the free assaults of enemies the most varied, with disestablishment and disendowment as a result, the first effect must be the falling away from the Church of those who either morally or intellectually, or both, are out of harmony with her.

Freedom of inquiry, with all other freedom, as it becomes more and more a settled institution, will more and more incline to diminish the effects of mere traditional adherence to family creed, and the passage to and fro will become more and more easy. Thus those with proclivities towards the Church, but who have been brought up from childhood external to her, will more readily find their true level, while those brought up within her pale, but who in spirit have revolted from her sway, will, by becoming manifestly external to her, cease to disgrace her or to lower the moral tone of her community.

Freedom of marriage, amongst other freedoms, will tend to produce strong hereditary predispositions, both for and in opposition to Christianity, but there will also be a most important action tending to favour the increase in number of those Christianly predisposed. This action is the stringent religious obligation imposed on married

Christians in no way to impede their natural multiplication, whilst the opposite practice is being widely urged outside the Church, and is likely to act as an increasing check on pagan propagation.

Moreover, as the two tendencies which have been here distinguished as "civicism" and "paganism" become disentangled and distinguished, an immense twofold gain must accrue to Christianity, if the modern movement continues so successfully and irresistibly that the tendency to revive the mediæval system becomes extinct. On the one hand, that activity which is now directed to a revival of mediævalism will be set free and applied to the protection of freedom against pagan despotism. On the other hand, nine tenths of the present hostility to the Church will have ceased when it is clearly and generally seen that no desire or intention of reviving mediævalism exists in it. Then those who are anti-theists, and fanatically opposed to Christianity in the interest of paganism, will stand alone against the combined opposition of Christians and advocates of freedom—that is, against those who can heartily combine on a basis of God-given natural right, whether that right be or be not supplemented and further enforced by divine revelation.

Thus it seems that when perfect free play is allowed, the Church must come to be more and more composed of naturally-selected citizens whose intellect fully approves her doctrines, and whose modes of life more or less fully harmonise with her precepts and counsels. Moreover, such citizens will naturally have their emotions more and more strongly excited, and their volitions rendered more and more vigorous, by those very actions which the struggle for existence renders needful in support and extension of that system to which they adhere, and which the fact of their adhesion under varying circumstances tends more and more to elicit.

Such, then, seems to be the answer afforded by the facts to the calm judicial inquirer who seeks to ascertain what must be the effect (through the operation of merely natural laws, upon the Christian Church) of the further continuance of the political portion of the great modern movement in the direction it has so long followed.

(1.) *The effect on Christianity will be to give increased coherence and strength to its organisation, and efficiency to its action.*

(2.) *The result of the conflict will depend, not on political changes, but on those matters which must occupy us hereafter—science and philosophy.*

He, however, who wishes to judge fully of the matter here treated should endeavour to place himself in imagination at the Churchman's standpoint, and consider how he might express himself as to the course of modern political evolution in relation to Christianity.

The Churchman might express his sentiments somewhat thus:

"The Church as a whole has never known retrogression or defeat since she first stepped forth from the upper chamber in Jerusalem, conquering and to conquer. The Church's progress is to be estimated not by the number of souls who externally profess belief in her, but by the number who obey her laws in a sufficient degree to obtain their salvation.

"When the Church, in mounting the throne with Constantine, obtained what in the eyes of the world was a startling triumph, she made no doubt a true and proper step in advance, but one attended with many concomitant disadvantages and dangers. In condescending to allow her sacred monogram to adorn imperial standards, and in permitting kings to sanctify their diadems with the sign of the Cross, gratitude was due from powers so favoured to the Church which granted them, not subservience from the mother and queen to the children she nourished and protected. In the words of the head of the Church in England, 'It is not the State which establishes the Church, it is the Church which establishes the State.'

"The barbaric tribes successively led under the Church's sway were providential agents in bringing about that glorious dawn of Church supremacy, the mediæval theocracy. But unavoidable defects attended that development. Vast numbers of the indifferent, the gross, the merely credulous, and the worldly, were led within the Church's fold by circumstances, accepted its doctrines unhesitatingly but unprofitably, since in them 'works' did not accompany 'faith,' and belief without charity, as Dr. Newman has so well shown, leads directly to superstition.

"The Christian mediæval system culminated in as near an approach to a universal theocracy as was then possible; but the world was manifestly quite unripe for a more perfectly developed condition, with (as we now know) its far larger area unchristianised, more than half undiscovered, and with a vast mass of latent paganism in the part which was externally Christianised.

"A great process of differentation and division of labour had necessarily to be gone through. For the perfection of society, philosophy, politics, science, and art, had to become the exclusive occupation of different minds, instead of remaining in the hands of the clergy, whose proper study is theology. These fields of activity could not be adequately cultivated without the devotion of many minds entirely and exclusively to one or other of them. Had Christians, especially those highly placed, been thoroughly imbued with the spirit of their religion, no doubt the necessary transformations might have taken place peacefully and without religious disruption, but the essentially papal character of the Church was not fully recognised, nor was it then experimentally known how by separation from the centre of spiritual life the supply of vital force is thereby necessarily cut off. The pagan principle of State supremacy, once effectually introduced, ran its logical and inevitable course fatally to the mediæval theocracy and the social system therewith connected. Providentially accompanying this movement has gone on a gradual perfecting of the Church's independent organism, and a greater and greater detachment of it from the State.

"The Church has willingly lent its support to the secular power, which, in return, has either sought perfidiously to bind it in golden chains, or has brutally spurned it, as now in Germany. This fortunate perfidy will enable the Church to escape the popular enmity which the State is sure, sooner or later, to incur, while its perfect organisation will enable it to survive and flourish the better for the pseudo-Christian State's downfall and replacement by a system of natural freedom for each individual citizen.

"This process of reinvigoration is already becoming patent. Since the clearly logical and Christian declarations of Boniface VIII., no pontiff has so uncompromisingly asserted the Church's claims as Pius IX.

"The completion of the anti-mediæval movement will only bring out yet more clearly what is but in effect and in other terms the proclamation and assertion of the supreme rights of conscience. But while the extent of the Church's success in the thirteenth century should not be over-stated, so also there is no cause for discouragement in the apparent reverses it has since undergone. Whether under the anti-papal revolts of the sixteenth century, or the anti-Christian revolutions of the eighteenth and nineteenth centuries, the same unvarying process of steadily increasing conquest has been, is, and will be incessantly going on, and this in spite of superficial appearances to the contrary. As to the first of these events (the sixteenth century revolt), the spread of the faith in the new world compensated for its restriction in the old, while its very restriction was the occasion of the more complete development of the faith in the area which retained it, where it became more intensely and consciously held. As to the second event, its wonderfully invigorating actions on those who remain Christians in France, Italy, Switzerland, and Germany, is before our eyes to-day.

"The manifest religious changes of the sixteenth century will ultimately turn out to have been really to the Church's advantage. Before then, the Church contained a mass of latent heresy and infidelity, while now the religious bodies external to the Church contain a mass of latent orthodoxy.

"This is especially the case amongst English-speaking Christians. The noble anti-Erastian passion of the sturdy Puritans, and their honest zeal against what they believed to be idolatry, were essentially most Catholic, as was also the heartfelt piety of the evangelican protest against the cold formalism of the established clergy of that time. The marvellous growth of high church views has resulted in a forest of new spires, in schools, convents, and pious institutions, far and wide in our land—proclaiming the deep and earnest nature of our religious progress. Even the very fanaticisms of 'sabbath observance' and 'bibliolatry' are replete with Catholic ascetic and devotional instincts, however misdirected.

"In the Protestant masses of to-day is contained an immense body of latent Catholicism, like some chemical substance in solution, which but requires a sudden change of temperature or the introduction of some foreign body to precipitate itself, or become manifest in a conspicuous crystallisation. The number of those who have really understood the Church and rejected her is infinitesimal, and article after article, and book after book, again and again show how profoundly she is misapprehended, and how the mass of the hostility directed against her is really directed not against her, but against that to which she also is no less opposed.

"Even the anarchic spirit of the 'Internationalists' is in one respect really vivified by a profound Christian spirit—the spirit of cosmopolitanism. They clearly see that a man who would sacrifice the welfare of the world to that of his country is only one degree less selfish than the man who would sacrifice his country to aggrandise his family. What was the very first step in the destruction of the Christian theocracy becomes thus condemned and reprobated by the logical descendants of such destroyers as Philip the Fair and Henry the Eighth.

"Of course that destructive action cannot be approved and can still less be aided by any sincere Christian. So to approve would be to repeat the error of De Lamennais. A separation of Church and State cannot be good save relatively through human perverseness. A union of Church and State is the natural and true ideal, and will spontaneously reappear (when once the world has been reconverted) through common consent. But Christianity is forbidden to propagate itself by the sword. The children of those who have thrown off her yoke and who are becoming more and more literally pagans cannot, *upon Church principles*, be religiously coërced or called on to accept that which, on account of honest prejudice, their reason is really unable to embrace. The Church absolutely condemns * the use of force when a nation has either not received or has once lost the faith.

"But although the crew of Bismarcks, Garibaldis, and Victor Emmanuels may be regarded as obscene creatures of rapine, nevertheless, hyænas and vultures have, after all, a useful and salutary function to execute, without their having any good intention in the acts they perform, or being a bit less unclean vultures and hyænas on account of the salutary nature of that function.

"A continuous action of six hundred years has not been permitted without good cause, and the changes effected,

---

* "Ad cœlum homines trahendos esse, non cogendos."—*Breviary Office for St. Augustine of Canterbury.*

however iniquitously brought about, have been providentially allowed and overruled for the full development of the Church in all its glory through the manifestation of its action in a world of full civic freedom.

"The pagan movement, which made its way by asserting and proclaiming freedom, is ending in an attempt at the most extreme and debasing of despotisms.

"The Christian movement, which progressed through strong assertion of authority, is ending, as it logically should do from its principles, in being the great supporter of individual freedom reposing upon conscience—'rights' answering to 'duties.'

"The long process of Christian integration having, in the Vatican Council, culminated in the complete organisation of supreme authority, the liberty of the individual regains full play—the restraint of conscientious fears as to possible ill effects of his utterances being removed by the recognition of a ready and infallible authority capable of rendering his well-meant but mistaken efforts harmless. Similarly, the whole hierarchical system of subordinate authority, down to the private confessor, being fully established, and the whole controlling agency necessary for the Church's stability having been completed, a freer play may be given to individual energies than for the centuries past during which that agency was developing and perfecting. If before, the energies and activities of Churchmen were unequal to those of their opponents, this relation will speedily be reversed, as Switzerland and Germany are beginning to show us. The missions of the Greeks and Latins with regard to the Church being mainly fulfilled, the vigorous Teutonic race has now to promote its peaceful triumph through individual energy in the arena of civic freedom.

"Judging then of the future by the past, changes to come will but bring out more and more the Church's true nature by gathering in the latent Catholicity of separated bodies, and by sloughing off such unworthy members as have, in the past, been retained in it by sloth, ignorance, or interest. It will thus necessarily become more and more conspicuous for the holiness of its members as compared with such of the population as is avowedly pagan and unbelieving. As the process of evolution has gone on from the inorganic world to the organic, from the vegetable to the animal, and from the simplest form of sentient life, through constantly increasing complexity, till the hour struck for the introduction of a rational animal into the world, so the evolution of humanity has proceeded, and is proceeding, from direct and simple conscious apprehensions to more and more reflex, self-conscious, and complex comprehensions. And this applies fully to the acceptance of the Christian Church. As it has been, so it will be. Of time there is no stint. The next glacial epoch is sufficiently remote. By the continuance, then, of this evolutionary process there is to be plainly discerned in the distant future a triumph of the Church compared with which that of mediæval Christendom was but a transient adumbration. A triumph brought about by moral means alone—by the slow process of exhortation, example, and individual conviction, after every error has been freely propagated, every denial freely made, and every rival system provided with a free field for its display. A triumph infinitely more glorious than any brought about by the sword, and fulfilling at last the old pre-Christian prophecies of the kingdom of God upon earth."

Such, perhaps, might be the Churchman's reply as to the position and prospects of Christianity, to those who oppose to him the phenomena of the last six centuries' change. Here it has been endeavoured dispassionately to estimate what, at the very utmost, must be the destructive effects on Christianity of the greatest amount of anti-theocratic change which can possibly be anticipated, and the answer has been that there is no reason to apprehend even its enfeeblement, still less its annihilation.

Nevertheless, we have yet but considered the political aspect of the great modern anti-mediæval movement. The scientific and, most important of all, the philosophic aspects of that movement remain to be considered. We may conclude that the political changes will be harmless to the Church, but it will manifestly be quite otherwise if either science or philosophy contradicts its dogmas.

Whatever the effect, however, one thing is certain—that science will address itself with greater and greater power to a constantly increasing circle of auditors, and will command an increasing number of cultivators and experts; and it is to be hoped that the same may be said also of philosophy.

If, then, either scientific and philosophic evolution is hostile to Christianity, the progress of such evolution must be fatal to it, and political evolution, by giving them increased liberty, must hasten their fatal effect. To these aspects of evolution then we must next address ourselves.

NOTE.

Some months after the above passage was first published, the views and expectations expressed in it were remarkably confirmed by three articles which appeared in the *Pall Mall Gazette*, in the numbers for December the 24th and 29th, 1874, and January 14th, 1875, respectively. From these articles the following passages may be cited:—

"DEMOCRACY AND THE ROMAN CATHOLIC CHURCH."

"Whether Monsignor Meglia did or did not say that, except in America, Belgium, and England, the Revolution was the only means by which the Roman Catholic Church could hope to recover her lost liberties, the idea is one which must at times present itself to the minds of the younger school of ecclesiastics. A new pope may acquiesce in, if he does not originate, a radical change of policy, and the next vacancy in the chair of Peter may hereafter be looked back to as the starting-point of a new fight for spiritual supremacy on the part of the Roman Catholic Church. It is plain to outside observers, whatever it may be to the Roman curia, that the old allies of the Church are no longer of any use to her. Kings and aristocracies are now only accidentally powerful. They succeed in so far as they interpret and adopt the great currents of popular sentiment. They fail whenever they try to maintain or bring back the system which since the French Revolution has everywhere been struck with incurable decay. Kingly support and court influence can now do but little even for those who can command them. Nor is it by any means certain that even if their hold upon the world were restored to them they would be disposed to exert it in favour of the Church. Courts and aristocracies naturally embody the ideas of the educated classes for the time being, and one great cause of the recent defeats of the Roman Catholic Church has been the general spread of irreligion, using the word in its most general sense, among the educated classes throughout Europe. The number of persons who disbelieve the Christian dogmas is probably greater than at any former time, and what is even more important to the matter in hand, it is becoming less and less fashionable to conceal their disbelief. Kings and nobles are no more proof against this tendency than other educated men, and in so far as they are influenced by it they would not be disposed to help the Church to regain her lost empire, even if they had power to do so. Indeed, in the improbable contingency of this power returning to them, they would almost certainly shrink from exercising it from their desire not to share in the unpopularity of the Church. If the Comte de Chambord were to become king of France, the first request his lay advisers would address to him would be to shake himself free from the priests. When the Roman Catholic Church awakes to the fact that those on whom it has so long leaned have neither their old strength nor their old willingness to use it for ecclesiastical objects, it cannot fail to see that it has only two alternatives to choose between. It must throw up the battle altogether, or it must seek for new alliances among those who have solid support to give.

"At first sight it must be admitted the prospect appears gloomy enough. All over Europe 'the Revolution' and hatred of the

Church are almost convertible terms. In France and Italy the democracy is only kept from slaughtering the clergy in cold blood by the fear of legal or military consequences. There are thousands of workmen in Paris to whom the murder of the Archbishop of Paris only suggests a regret that he was not shot for being a priest instead of being shot as a hostage, and this feeling is reproduced with more or less accuracy in every large town on the Continent. There is very little of this sort of fanaticism in England; but even here, if Mr. Bradlaugh had his will, the priests might have a bad time. It is to a democracy largely subject to these influences that the Church must make its appeal. But this hatred of the Church in the minds of the working classes is only partially due to the cause which has generated a modified form of the same feeling in the minds of the educated classes. Disbelief in its coarser shapes no doubt prevails among them to a very great extent, but even this disbelief has probably a political rather than an intellectual origin. They disbelieve because they hate, rather than hate because they disbelieve. The main cause of democratic antagonism to the Roman Catholic Church has been its alliance for so many centuries with those whom the democracy regards as its oppressors. In every struggle the Church has been on the side of the powers that be. It has not only become associated by this means with the unpopularity which attaches to these powers, it has even attracted the largest share of it to its own shoulders. The Church was hated in the first instance because it supported the privileged classes, and one of the principal reasons why the privileged classes are now hated is that they are suspected of wishing well to the Church.

"Now the change of policy foreshadowed in the speech attributed to Monsignor Meglia would strike at the root of the hatred felt by democrats towards the Church. The accumulated detestation of centuries would remain, but no fresh additions would be made to the store. And when the source of supply is cut off, it is remarkable how soon a feeling of this kind begins to decay. The recollections of past wrongs grow faint in the light of present services. The political tendencies now in action will help on this process of oblivion. The French *noblesse* under Louis XVI. had for the most part ceased to oppress the poor, but they retained the property which had been the visible symbol of oppression, and they suffered not so much for what they did as for what they had. The drift of contemporary legislation promises to set the Church entirely free from a similar danger. She will no longer wear the livery of the secular powers from whom she has parted company. There will be nothing in her aspect to remind her enemies of her ancient wealth or of her ancient grandeur. Besides this, the foe from whom she has most to fear is certain to make itself many adversaries, and every one of these adversaries will be a possible ally of the Church. The form of despotism which is most in favour at present, and most likely to become stronger in the immediate future, is the despotism of a highly centralised State. Communities surrender their freedom in return for unity and strength at home, and prestige abroad. For a time all goes on smoothly, and the subjects of the State are never tired of contemplating the system which they have themselves helped to build up. By-and-by these very same people begin to feel oppressed by their own creation. Resisting minorities start up in all directions; and the more resolutely they are put down, the more disposed they are to make common cause with all who share their slavery and their desire for emancipation. The Roman Catholic Church will have singular advantages in dealing with this temper. Its soldiers will have nothing to lose. If they die in the conflict, they leave no children to suffer from the loss of a father. Wherever their services are needed a subsistence is secured to them, and the enthusiasm which springs up in the field soon learns to desire nothing more. Under changed names and new conditions the Church will once more appear on the side of the weak against the strong, of the poor against the rich, of individual liberty against a tyrannical system. These are strong titles to democratic support, and though the sympathies of the democracy are at present on the side of the State, which they hope hereafter to mould at their pleasure, against the Church, which they cannot mould at all, the situation may undergo a radical change if the State becomes the inflexible and the Church the most flexible element in modern society.

"It has always been found that causes which have an emotional basis attract a far greater number of supporters and exercise a much firmer hold over them than causes which have only a basis of reason. So long as slavery in the United States was combated on economical or political grounds, its defenders had no reason to fear the attack. If they were unable to answer the arguments brought against them, they could comfort themselves by thinking that it did not matter whether they were answered or not. But when the abolitionist party lifted the question into the sphere of emotion, and denounced slavery and the constitution which permitted slavery on the plea of owing obedience to a higher law than any of man's making, the whole character of the controversy was altered, and slavery was doomed just when its strength seemed greatest. There is no organisation which can command emotion with so much certainty of evoking it as the Roman Catholic Church, and of all emotions the religious emotion is the strongest when thoroughly aroused.

"We have already indicated one or two of the grounds which make it probable that the present attitude of the Roman Catholic Church towards democracy will hereafter be completely changed. Some others still remain to be mentioned. In modern times—ever since, that is, the existing State system of Europe began to grow up—the Roman Catholic Church has been the most conservative of all institutions. But to suppose that it must remain what it is when the reasons for being what it is are at an end would be to underrate the ability which ecclesiastics have at various times displayed, and may very possibly display again.

"Supposing the Roman Catholic clergy to be convinced that their best if not their only chance of regaining their spiritual influence lies in an appeal to the democracy, their organisation and position would give them many advantages in making it. Their singular detachment from those family ties which make men fearful of running great risks has already been referred to. Their detachment from local ties would enable them to pursue a uniform policy in different countries and under different circumstances. In some cases they would be connected by birth with the classes whose temper they would have to study, and whose interests they would have to further. The example of Ireland may serve to show how intensely popular a clergy sprung from the people can become under favourable conditions. It seems probable that the Roman Catholic clergy will be more and more recruited from two sources—the lower classes, among whom traditional belief is still strong, and those of the upper classes who dislike the political system under which they live, and will consequently take orders with the desire to injure it in every way that presents itself. An appeal to the democracy will commend itself on different grounds to both these groups. With the first it will be instinctive; with the second it will be the result of calculation. It will not be enough, however, for the clergy to be convinced that the interest of the Church suggests an appeal to the democracy. The fact that you have an obvious motive for offering your services to a man with whom you have hitherto been on bad terms is apt to make him the less inclined to listen. Nor will it be enough for the clergy to be possessed of an organisation which will give them many advantages in making such an appeal. This, too, may only serve to put the democracy on their guard. Besides both these qualifications, there is wanted an enthusiasm on the part of the clergy which shall carry them over the hostility, the coldness, the suspicions with which their overtures are certain to be received in the first instance. Is there anything in the character or history of the Roman Catholic Church which is calculated to arouse this enthusiasm in its members?

"To answer this question fully would be to survey the whole field of ecclesiastical history. But, to note one or two only of the many points which suggest themselves, there is in the first place the essentially democratic origin of the Church. Whenever a Roman Catholic priest stands before the altar or mounts the pulpit, there hangs opposite to him the crucified form of One who was born in a stable, who grew to manhood in a carpenter's shed, whose chosen associates were poor men gaining a precarious livelihood by fishing, who wandered about without a roof to shelter Him, who was in constant conflict with all the traditional and accepted authorities of His nation, and who finally suffered death at their hands. What associations can be more likely to suggest democratic ideas to enthusiastic minds sprung, it may be, from poor parents, and themselves waging a continual warfare with the secular powers? The religion thus founded was the heir of an older faith which in its noblest development was an eminent protest against arrogance and oppression. 'Go to now, ye rich men, weep and howl,' though it occurs in an apostolic epistle, reproduces exactly the spirit of the Hebrew prophets. St. Paul's teaching lends itself to a similar application. A great orator who had persuaded himself that the success of his preaching depended on his carrying the multitude with him would hardly desire a better text than 'God hath chosen the weak things of the world to confound the things which are mighty; and base things of the world, and things which are despised, yea, and things which are not, to bring to nought things that are.' At present he would be hampered in handling his subject. He is not on the whole desirous of disturbing the existing order of secular affairs, and he would therefore have to explain that St. Paul's words were to be taken in a strictly spiritual sense. But assume him to have become a declared enemy of the existing order of secular affairs, and so to be emancipated from the restrictions which now fetter his eloquence, and he will have a vantage-ground from which to move democratic passion such as no merely secularist preacher is likely to share. The clergy need not even go so far back as the origin of their religion. The history of its youth and manhood is full of associations which point in the same direction. The glory of the mediæval Church is the resistance which it offered to tyranny of every kind. The typical bishop of those times is always upholding a righteous cause against kings and emperors, or exhorting masters to let their slaves go free, or giving sanctuary to harassed fugitives, or protecting the infant town against some neighbouring feudal lord, or inspiring the villagers whom their lord has deserted to make head against a piratical inroad, or joining with the better disposed barons in setting bounds to kingly aggression. What is true of the bishops is true in a still more eminent degree of the religious orders. Whether they aimed at guiding men by putting wealth to noble uses, or by neglecting it altogether, their object was equally to identify themselves with the poor. They are not likely soon to have another opportunity of playing the former part, but the occasions for the latter can never be denied them. If to belong to a religious order were made a capital offence in every country in Europe, it would not prevent the formation of secret societies, whose sole external symbol would be the greater readiness of their members to spend their substance upon others rather than upon themselves. There is enough in these considerations to excite enthusiasm, provided that other conditions are favourable. In appealing to the democracy, the Roman Catholic clergy would, in form at least, be reviving the best traditions of the Church. There will be nothing strange in their persuading themselves that power may be best recovered by boldly resorting to the methods which originally gained it.

"We certainly do not look forward to any incongruous alliance between the Roman Catholic Church and the Reds. To the extreme revolutionary party on the continent politics have become a religion, and the cardinal articles of that religion are probably held with as much fanaticism as can be commanded by the Roman Catholic Church itself. Supposing the Church to take the line we have indicated, we should rather regard it as a rival power bidding against the Reds for the friendship of the poorer classes of society. The Church would offer them equal sympathy, alloyed with less of that desire for personal aggrandisement which the poor are so ready to attribute to leaders of their own class. It would be quite as little hampered by any stereotyped reverence for economical laws. Ordinary politicians are disturbed if they become convinced that a particular line of action is opposed to the growth of capital. They are so accustomed to associate the well-being of a nation with its material progress, that a state of things which does not further the latter can hardly in their eyes tend to further the former. The Red Republican has emancipated himself from this tendency to link together the two ideas, and the genuine ecclesiastic has never been subject to it. For different reasons capital is scarcely less hateful to the one than to the other, and we are not at all sure that the doctrine that property is a trust held for the benefit of the poor may not prove as attractive to the cestuique trust as the rival doctrine that property is only legitimate when it has been distributed among the poor. Be this as it may, this is the attitude which we have supposed the Roman Catholic Church to take up—not striving to win over, or fancying that it can win over, the Reds, but offering to that great mass of poor men and women who are as yet neither Reds nor Catholics in any very definite sense, a creed as full of sympathy for their sufferings and on the whole less tied down to promises which those who make them cannot perform. We do not deny that the view which says, 'Why should we resign ourselves to the endurance of evils for which we shall never get any compensation?' has many attractions for energetic spirits, and at times when resignation is not the only course open. But in the long run it has always been found that sufferings and injustices are not removed by a resolution not to submit to them ; and whenever this discovery is made, there will always be a chance for the view which preaches submission to inevitable evils in the belief that they will be redressed hereafter."

CHAPTER IV.

SCIENTIFIC EVOLUTION.

IN the second chapter of this essay, an attempt was made to investigate the probable effect on Christianity of the further development of the great modern process of social evolution. It was therein stated that a trustworthy result could be arrived at only after considering (1) the *political*, (2) the *scientific*, and (3) the *philosophic* aspects of the question. As yet our inquiry has been limited to the political aspect alone, the others being deferred for subsequent consideration. The result so far arrived at has been that the political evolutionary process tends to increase the coherence and strength of the Christian organism, and to give greater efficiency to its action, by occasioning a series of internal integrating processes responsive to external disintegrating influences. Nevertheless a reservation was made as to the possible effects of scientific and philosophic evolution, to the effect that if contradiction thence arose such evolution must be fatal, while political change (by giving increased liberty of action) must hasten the final catastrophe. It remains then to consider the scientific and philosophic aspects of contemporary evolution in their relationship to Christianity, the subject being treated now, as in the preceding chapters, altogether without reference to the truth of that religion, and from the standpoint of natural science only.

The accelerated advance of physical science is the "commonplace" of our day. That it will address itself with augmenting power to increasing audiences is certain. Not less certain is it that, as before pointed out, theological questions are more and more calling forth zeal and energy in regions where a quarter of a century ago apathy and stagnation largely prevailed. Manifest, again, to the most cursory observer is the wide divergence of views and sentiments between large numbers of those more especially devoted to one or the other of these fields of activity. In the first chapter it was sought to pourtray and symbolise this divergence as concretely embodied in a mediæval abbey and a modern museum. How marked such divergence appears to the average middle-class mind in England to-day is evidenced by the contrast drawn by the *Times* between the British pilgrimage to Paray-le-Monial and the succeeding British Association meeting. It was evident that, in the writer's opinion, there would be more or less inconsistency in any one taking part with full sympathy in both those gatherings.

To those who think that such divergence of sentiment has its foundation in the intellect and is the expression of a real and necessary *rational* divergence, the effect of the further progress of evolution cannot be doubtful. Those thinkers will also naturally desire the complete and final overthrow of a superstition clogging the wheels of scientific progress, and will justly be moved to discourage (in all ways not conflicting with the equal rights of their fellow-citizens to liberty of conscience) a system they deem to be in contradiction with reason. On the other hand, there are those who are convinced that this divergence is not fundamentally a *rational* one at all, but, except where volition intervenes, the result of feebleness of imagination, absence of due mental flexibility, or simply of ignorance or prejudice. The author of this essay can at least testify that he has met with several, in many respects highly-gifted minds, who have had personal experience of this relative impotency, and who have only after many efforts, and sometimes wide oscillations, succeeded in effecting the mental synthesis referred to.

Yet the conflict at present existing between the two schools of thought is, as was earlier pointed out, the result of a gradual and steady growth through preceding centuries, and is, whatever be the result, likely for a time yet further to become intensified, from two special causes. One of these (1) is the action of the principle of the division of labour. The other (2) is the special character of some physical science teaching. The principle of the *division of labour* renders necessary the application of one man's almost entire energy to a more and more restricted field of scientific labour. Only intellectual giants can now hope for eminence in widely remote areas of study and research. To take an example from one science, men have not only almost ceased to be general zoologists, and become ornithologists, entomologists, &c., as the case may be; but we hear now of lives being devoted to the study of small sections of natural orders, and that this naturalist is a *Carabidist*,* and that a *Curculionist*,† while a German naturalist has even published a quarto volume, with large plates and numerous tables, the whole being devoted to the anatomy of the lower part of the hindmost bone of the skull of the carp!

Now physical science must continue, not only to grow in complexity as well as mass, but also to diffuse itself over an increasing area. The general diffusion of modern instruction will hereafter render a certain acquaintance with the facts and most approved theories of science the common property of all who have the least pretension to be deemed "educated," and influences as yet active, but in a very limited field, must sooner or later become all but universal. At the same time the clergy, diminished in relative number through the consequences of the Renaissance movement, will come to have less and less time to spare for any special acquisitions in physical science, and far from monopolising the physical knowledge of their time (as was the case in the

---

* *i.e.*, devoted to that family of beetles termed *Carabidæ*.
† *i.e.*, devoted to the long-snouted beetles termed *Curculionidæ*.

early part of the Middle Ages), they must have even less and less chance of often occupying distinguished positions in the scientific arena, such as those filled by numerous continental *abbés* before the epoch of the great French Revolution. Besides relative numerical decrease in the clergy and the increasing sub-division of the field of physical science labour just spoken of, a simultaneous growth in theological science must render the attainment of eminence in any one of the more and more restricted branches of physical science still more difficult, and all but a matter of impossibility to a clergy devoted to a theology which, whether true or false, is also ever increasing in complexity as well as mass by a development responsive to the actions of surrounding influences. Thus it appears to be inevitable that as time goes on we shall come to have a population more and more imbued with physical science, and at the same time a clergy less and less raised above the mass of the laity as regards a knowledge of such science. These conditions, accompanying as they will a growing appreciation of physical science, must favour the already wide-spread belief in a real antagonism of reason between science and Christianity. The mere existence of such a belief (coinciding as it does, with anti-Christian tendencies which it helps to intensify) cannot but produce results, temporarily, at least, very hurtful to the Christian organism, since it tends altogether to divert from the examination of the Church's claims inquiring minds which otherwise might perhaps find her acceptable to their mental states, and to destroy the belief of others who, from a very distinct cause, may be specially susceptible to such influence. Hence there seems but little reason to expect that the existing wide-spread connection between familiarity with physical science and disbelief in Christianity will, for a considerable period, diminish—to anticipate, that is, that a movement which has been gradually growing in strength for six hundred years is likely soon to be arrested. So far, then, the scientific aspect of contemporary evolution appears hostile to the growth and influence of the Church. Yet we may find hereafter (when we have considered the second cause) compensating actions leading to results quite opposite to those which have as yet appeared.

The second cause of hostility was stated to be "*the special character of some physical science teaching.*"

Physical science occupies itself with the phenomenal universe as far as accessible to our senses, the collocations of causes in the visible world, together with the laws of their action—in short, with the co-existences and successions of phenomena, from mathematics and sidereal astronomy to biology and sociology.*

---

* Mr. G. H. Lewes (" Problems of Life and Mind ") professes to embrace " metaphysics " within the range of science. He does so, however, merely by calling " metaphysical " certain physical conceptions by which phenomena are mentally connected in scientific minds,

Theology occupies itself with an asserted noumenal universe, inaccessible to our senses, the collocation of causes in such an invisible world, together with the laws of their action—in short, with the relations of spiritual entities from God down to the human soul.

Such being the case—the two domains being so distinct—it seems difficult to conceive how *any* development of physical science can possibly conflict with natural theology, and yet the fact is patent that it is very often supposed to do so. It is true, of course, that Christian theology does make a limited number of assertions with respect to certain facts (such, *e.g.*, as those contained in the Church's creed), which were at one time subjects of sensible experience. It is manifest, therefore, that if science, *e.g.*, history, could demonstrate any one of these assertions to be false, such science must be not merely hostile but deadly in its action on Christianity. No writer, however, as yet has even claimed to have established a demonstration of the kind. Indeed, all competent minds have recognised the fact that physical science, apart from *à priori* philosophical conceptions, must be alike incapable of disproving them or of establishing their impossibility. Nevertheless, there are always more or less widely diffused among Christians various "pious opinions" (as they are termed), which

---

and by bestowing the new name "metempirics" on that which has been hitherto universally called "metaphysics."

are often held with great tenacity, although forming no part of what the Church affirms as divinely revealed. This it is which is the region of conflict, and it is strewn over with weapons more or less hastily caught up by assailants as possessing a fatal efficiency and afterwards abandoned in disappointment. Not that the weapons were pointless or their wielders unskilful, but that by the destruction of an encumbering delusion they conferred benefits on the cause which was the real object of their attack. In England, both the assailants and the supporters of popular Christianity are peculiarly liable to become involved in such contests. They are thus liable because of the often startling ignorance of Christian dogma amongst the former, and the prevalence of a certain peculiar superstition amongst the latter. This superstition is the somewhat grotesque belief that the ever freshly surging questions of theology—presenting themselves in new aspects in each succeeding age—are to be answered by revelation indeed, but through a printed book, and not through some living authority capable of addressing to each succeeding epoch its specially fitting response. Nevertheless, not in England alone, but throughout the civilised world, such conflicts have raged from time to time, and two noteworthy ones may be here suitably adverted to.

It is not probable that physical science will again be the occasion of so great a disturbance to prevalent "pious beliefs" as when it first introduced heliocentric astronomy to the Christian world.* The primitive cosmo-

---

* On this subject Dr. Newman observes :—" When the Copernican system first made progress, what religious man would not have been tempted to uneasiness, or at least fear of scandal, from the seeming contradiction which it involved to some authoritative tradition of the Church and the declaration of Scripture? It was generally received, as if the apostles had expressly delivered it, both orally and in writing, that the earth was stationary, and that the sun was fixed in a solid firmament which whirled round the earth. After a little time, however, and on full consideration, it was found that the Church had decided next to nothing on questions such as these, and that physical science might range in this sphere of thought almost at will, without fear of encountering the decisions of ecclesiastical authority. Now, besides the relief which it afforded to Catholics to find that they were to be spared this addition, on the side of cosmology, to their many controversies already existing, there is something of an argument in this circumstance in behalf of the divinity of their religion. For it surely is a very remarkable fact, considering how widely and how long one certain interpretation of these physical statements in Scripture had been received by Catholics, that the Church should not have formally acknowledged it. Looking at the matter in a human point of view, it was inevitable that she should have made that opinion her own. But now we find, on ascertaining where we stand, in the face of the new sciences of these latter times, that, in spite of the bountiful comments, which from the first she has ever been making on the sacred text, as it is her duty and her right to do, nevertheless she has never been led formally to explain the texts in question, or to give them an authoritative sense which modern science may question. Nor was this escape a mere accident, or what will more religiously be called a providential event, as is shown by a passage of history in the Dark Age itself. When the glorious St. Boniface, Apostle of Germany, great in sanctity, though not in secular knowledge, complained to the Holy See that St. Virgilius taught the existence of the antipodes, the

logical conception had in its favour alike the convictions of the majority of the learned, the language of books revered as sacred, and the enormous force of a habit of mind unbroken for untold ages. Yet the result of the universal acceptance of the new astronomy, so far from destroying the Christian Church (as it is asserted it would have destroyed Hindooism), has been to show that it was in fact prepared beforehand for the greatest change of cosmological conception which the world has yet seen.

The second instance is that of the apparent conflict between evolutionary biology and Christian dogma, and indeed, no better test question as to the effect of scientific progress on Christianity could well be devised. The general acceptance, till modern times, of one special view of creative action, together with the unhesitating consent of almost all men of science as to the indefinite durability of specific characters, made it in the highest degree unlikely that authoritative Christian teaching, in early mediæval times, should have laid down principles rendering the assimilation of evolutionary natural history by

---

Holy See apparently evaded the question, not indeed siding with the Irish philosopher, which would have been going out of its place, but passing over in a manner not revealed a philosophical opinion" (Lectures on University Subjects, p. 279). With how much even greater force do not these remarks apply to the Church's action respecting belief as to the mode of creation of animal and vegetable forms.

theology not only possible but easy and natural. Nevertheless, it has been shown* that such assimilation is thus easy and natural, and so far as the present writer is aware, not even an attempt at a reply has yet been made to the statements and reasonings there brought forward. Christians may surely be pardoned if they consider this a proof case; and assert that the religion that has borne this strain will bear any that physical science can bring to bear upon it. It might also be similarly shown that various other scientific questions (by some supposed to have a tendency conflicting with Christian dogma)—such as the antiquity of man, the phenomena of savage life, the necessity of nervous action to human thought, etc.—are beside the question, are indifferent matters in this relation, and necessarily futile as a basis of attack on the Church, and that, of course, whether the Church's claims be well or ill founded. On the other hand, it would not be difficult to show that there is a tendency in modern science—notably in biology—to direct men's minds in the *opposite* direction. That is to say, to direct them towards conceptions once generally current,† but which have, during the last three centuries, gradually passed

---

* *Contemporary Review*, January, 1872, and the last chapter of "Lessons from Nature" (Murray, 1876).

† This is particularly striking in Mr. Lewes's "Problems of Life and Mind," although reference thereto will come better under the head of philosophic than of scientific evolution.

out of general consciousness and become "forgotten" rather than "rejected."

Such being the relations existing between Christianity and physical science, What it may be asked, can be the peculiar character of science teaching which tends to prolong the hostility which has so long occupied us?

Shortly: then, it is not the science teaching itself, it is the metaphysics which consciously or unconsciously happen so often to have been propagated with it. In considering the teaching of physical science, two very different things require to be well distinguished: (1) the facts as to the co-existences and sequences of phenomena; and (2) the special system of philosophy which such facts may be made use of to inculcate.

Physical science, being by its very nature occupied exclusively with phenomenal conceptions, must plainly be capable of adaptation to, or explanation by, more than one system of philosophy; and that it is so experience proves. The Berkeleyan, the Kantist, the peripatetic, and the materialist find no difficulty in presenting the facts of science in harmony with their respective views. We have seen that physical science itself must be simply indifferent as regards Christianity, but the very reverse is of course the case with the materialistic or pantheistic philosophical systems so often associated with it. The existence of such association is notorious, and the names of Vogt and Büchner may well be quoted as prominent inculcators of such teaching. With loud professions of man's necessary ignorance is often joined a confident assertion as to the details of that course which would certainly be followed by a being of infinite power, wisdom, and goodness, did such a being exist.

For one of the latest examples of the spirit of this teaching we are indebted to Dr. Struther, who propounded at Bradford an argument which has been* thus summarised:—" Because one or two individuals have died from the impactation of cherry-stones in the appendix vermiformis, therefore there is no God." We have no evidence of the possibility having occurred to that gentleman that an indefinite number of final causes for the structure in question may (though unthought of by him) have preceded the existence of matter at all, and that amongst them might be the intellectual and moral effects of its contemplation on the minds of different men.

The specimen cited is typical, because the religious doctrines directly and openly, or obliquely and covertly attacked in connection with the teaching referred to, are not those of Christianity specially, but of theism generally. The direction of attack has indeed greatly changed since the epoch of the "deists." It is now pretty generally admitted, with regard to "Christianity" and "theism" that arguments really telling against the first are in their

---

* In *Nature*, Oct. 16, 1873, vol. viii., No. 207, p. 509.

logical consequences fatal also to the second, and that a *Deus unus et remunerator* once admitted, an antecedent probability for a revelation must be conceded.

Examples of popular materialistic science teaching have been elsewhere given by the present writer,* and their tendencies pointed out.

The teaching cited appeared capable of being summed up as follows:

" I. Temporal happiness is the one rational aim of life.

" II. A postive belief in God and a future life is an unwarrantable superstition.

" III. Virtue and pleasure are synonymous, for in root and origin they are identical.

" IV. Men are essentially but brutes, no differences of kind dividing them.

" V. The Cause of all things has not personality, and consequently neither feeling, nor intelligence, nor will.

" VI. All who pretend to teach religion are impostors or dupes.

" VII. Our physical science teachers are the supreme exponents of truth, and the ultimate arbiters of all actions.

" VIII. There is no such thing as real merit or demerit, as all our actions are absolutely determined for us, and free will is the most baseless of delusions."

Amongst the most recent manifestations of scientific

---

* See " Lessons from Nature " (Murray, 1876), chap. xiii., pp. 386–403.

materialism may be cited Professor Haeckel's History of Creation.

Professor Haeckel is a very instructive writer, because his zeal for materialistic pantheism is so fiery that it hurries him sometimes into antitheistic deductions from supposed facts which later investigations prove to have been fictions (*e.g.*, the supposed organism *Bathybius Haeckelii*, too probably but a sea mare's-nest, discovered by Professor Huxley, and appropriately named by him after his German *alter ego*), sometimes into a ludicrously exaggerated estimate of the philosophical or theological consequences of elementary truths; *e.g.*, those of development.

This writer tells us (vol. i., p. 179): "The soul of man, just as the soul of animals, is a purely mechanical activity, the sum of molecular phenomena of motion in the particles of the brain." Again he is translated as saying (p. 237): "The widely spread dogma of the freedom of the will is from a scientific point of view altogether untenable; every physiologist who scientifically investigates the activity of the will, must of necessity arrive at the conviction that *in reality the will is never free*, but is always determined by external or internal influences."

The animus of the author and his freedom from prejudice in judging is made manifest by the praise he gives to Mr. Darwin's hypothesis for its antitheistic tendency, and by mentioning (p. 115) "as a special merit of Lamarck, that he endeavoured to prove the *development of the human race* from other primitive ape-like mammals."

He speaks (p. 75) of the time "when man, first developing out of the monkey state, began for the first time to think MORE closely (!) about himself, and about the origin of the world around him"! It would be interesting to catch one of our monkeys in the Regent's Park thinking "loosely" about the origin of the world, and to photograph its aspect while so occupied.

Very amusing, however, are Haeckel's remarks as to the wonderful results which are to follow a general acquaintance with the simple facts of human embryonic development, with which mysteries he naïvely imagines "speculative philosophers" and "theologians" are not acquainted. He tells us (p. 295), "These facts are not calculated to excite approval among those who assume a thorough difference between man and the rest of nature"! Surely it is time that a man like Haeckel, who has done good service with respect to anatomical and zoological facts, should cease to give utterance to such mere *enfantillage*.

The wonderful manner, however, in which his mental vision is, not so much obscured as inverted, by prejudice (which we may hope is due rather to defective education than to bad will), is made unmistakably plain by the following passage from his "Generelle Morphologie der Organismen," vol. ii., p. 436, in which he declares that some brutes are the intellectual superiors of many men, in that they (the brutes) are not cramped in their mental action by dogmatic religious beliefs. His words are, speaking of Darwinian controversies :—

"In dieser Frage stossen wir wiederum auf die heftigste Opposition gerade bei denjenigen Menschen, welche durch ihre unvollkommnere Verstandes—Entwickelung oft selbst hinter den höheren Thieren zurückbleiben. Dies gilt nicht allein von den niederen Menschen-Rassen, sondern auch von vielen Individuen der höchsten Rassen, und selbst von solchen, bei denen Man vermuthen sollte, dass die Masse erworbener Kenntnisse ihr Denkvermögen geschärft habe. Besonders interessant sind gerade in dieser Beziehung zahlreiche Aeusserungen von Gegnern der Descendenz-Theorie, welche oft in wahrhaft erstaunlicher Weise einen Mangel an natürlicher, klarer und scharfer Gedanken-Bildung und Gedanken-Verbindung bezeugen, der sie entschieden unter die verständigeren Hunde, Pferde und Elephanten stellt. Da diese Thiere meistens nicht durch die alpenhohen Gebirgsketten von Dogmen und Vorurtheilen beschränkt werden, welche das Denken der meisten Menschen von Jugend an in schiefe Bahnen lenken, so finden wir bei ihnen nicht selten richtigere und natürlichere Urtheile, als sie namentlich bei den 'Gelehrten' anzutreffen sind."

"As to this question, we have to contend against the most vehement opposition of those men who, by their imperfect intellectual development, often remain behind even the higher brutes. This is the case, not only with the lower, but also with many individuals of the highest order of human beings, and even with men whose wits we might have expected to find sharpened by the mass of their acquired knowledge. Especially interesting, in this relation, are the numerous utterances of anti-evolutionists, which often display in an astounding manner a want of aptitude for the clear and sharp formation and association of ideas ; by which want they come to rank decidedly beneath the more intelligent dogs, horses, and elephants. For these animals, *for the most part*, are not hemmed in by Alpine summits of dogmas and prejudices, which lead the thought of most men, from youth upwards, into devious bye-paths. Thus we not unfrequently find in such animals more just and natural judgments than we find in many men, especially in men of letters."

This (temporary and accidental) association of certain metaphysical teaching with physics,* must naturally tend

---

* An instructive instance occurred not long ago, on the part of one of our leading thinkers, of the assumption that a protest against such association must necessarily be unscientific. Mr. Gladstone, in an address given at Liverpool, had remarked : " Upon the ground of what is termed evolution, God is relieved of the labour of creation ; in the name of unchangeable laws, He is discharged from governing the world." Upon this he was taxed by Mr. Herbert Spencer " *Study of Sociology*," p. 393) as " conspicuously making himself the exponent of the anti-scientific view," as regarding as " irreligious any explanation of nature which dispenses with immediate

to make Christian ministers assume a jealous if not hostile attitude towards physical science, and also to alienate a certain number of their disciples from them. Surely there

divine superintendence," and as overlooking "the fact that the doctrine of gravitation, with the entire science of physical astronomy, is open to the same charge" as the doctrine of evolution. Mr. Spencer is one of the last men to make an ill-considered charge, least of all against a thinker of a school opposed to his own, and it is therefore interesting to find that he does not appear to contemplate even the possibility of right being on Mr. Gladstone's side. That gentleman has written to vindicate himself from the charge of hostility to science, and to say (*Contemporary Review*, December, 1873, p. 163) that his complaint is that the functions of the Almighty as Creator and Governor of the world are denied upon grounds, which . . . "appear to" him "utterly and manifestly insufficient to warrant such denial." But in fact what Mr. Gladstone said was most true and just—not in opposition to Mr. Spencer (who is open to criticism of another kind), but in opposition to the general tendency and effects on men's minds of the teaching in vogue—an effect boastingly announced by outspoken adherents. Caro (" L'Idée de Dieu," p. 47) observes : " Science conducts God with honour to its frontiers, thanking Him for His provisional services." Mr. Gladstone said no more than this ! But there is a further misunderstanding. To explain the conditions of the solar system, considered with reference to physical science alone, the laws of astronomy are of course sufficient ; but to adequately explain such conditions as parts of a great whole of which our own intellectual faculties form a portion, astronomical laws are *not* sufficient, according to the teaching of a definite school of philosophy which claims Aristotle for its founder. Therefore, according to that philosophy, to say that a full recognition of the "doctrine of evolution" dispenses with "immediate divine superintendence," whether in the moon's motion or in the fall of a projectile, would be absurd. But this is the very error into which the unlearned are apt to fall, and this is the absurdity against which Mr. Gladstone meant, no doubt, to protest—the absurdity, that is, of supis not merely much excuse for, but merit in such hostility, when the nature, in their eyes, of two conflicting interests is considered. For any one who accepts not a revelation, but only natural religion, must regard *religious* and *physical* truth as possessing no common measure, just as the grandeur and beauty of Saturn's rings and the grandeur and beauty of an heroic act of generous self-denial cannot be compared together. To such acceptors of revelation, questions as to "the age of the world" or the "law of new specific origins" must appear trivial details when weighed in the balance with such questions as, "Is the human will really free?" "Are our efforts after virtue lovingly responded to by an Infinite Being, who knows every secret of our hearts so intimately, that the closest human scrutiny is but an utterly inadequate

---

posing that "gravitation" or "evolution" if accepted are not "utterly and manifestly insufficient" to account for the phenomena, apart from Divine action, when such phenomena are considered as part of a universe made up of spiritual as well as of material existences. It seems then, evident, that Mr. Gladstone, in the passage first cited, speaks as the adherent of one school of philosophy, while Mr. Spencer speaks as the adherent of another. The claims of these rival philosophies cannot be stated in this note, but whether the peripatetic be true or false, all who hold it have a perfect right to speak as Mr. Gladstone spoke, without on that account having one fraction the less of love for physical science or of desire for knowledge of the laws of the phenomenal universe, from "gravitation" to the sociological value of the art of music and the *true* teleological relations of the "locomotive" and the "fiddle" respectively.

symbol of it?" "Has a revelation been made; and if so, what are its contents?"

If we before thought it just that those convinced of scientific truths should be moved to discourage a system they deem to be in contradiction with reason "from the scientific point of view, we must surely also think it just that those convinced of philosophic truths should be moved to discourage a system they deem to be in contradiction with reason," from the philosophic point of view. So long, therefore, and in so far as pantheism or materialism are associated with physical science, those who uphold theism will be more or less opposed to such science while so associated. Thus it seems that the two special causes considered act together to prolong the already long-standing antagonism between physics and theology.

Yet of any real antagonism between them we have found no trace, even in such a proof case as the application of the evolutionary hypothesis to the appearance of new species of animals. Physical science should then be considered, alike by the philosophic Christian and anti-Christian, as neutral and indifferent. The question whether the philosophies in vogue accept and collocate the facts of science better than any other philosophy, cannot be considered till we come to the question of philosophic evolution. Meanwhile, it appears that it is only possible for the advance of science to influence Christianity through such philosophy as may be incorporated with it. Philosophy affords, then, the real battle-ground for the contending forces, and it is on that all-important field that the future of Europe, the endurance of an existing social system, and the fate of Christianity must be decided.

But we may ask, Has not the advance of science itself an indirect effect upon the struggle? Does this advance tend to hinder or promote the study of philosophy? If it does do either, then, of course, it indirectly aids in the conflict, though itself inoperative directly. Now every physical science is, when once its study has been fairly begun, intensely interesting. Most popular sciences, such as zoology, botany, geology, etc., are followed with comparative facility, and are, to most minds, far easier than philosophical study, where the intellect has so constantly to be turned in upon itself. Yet from the limitations imposed by their very nature on the physical sciences, they tend to leave the minds of the more inquiring (and as education becomes diffused, of a greater number) with an unsatisfied craving after deeper explanations—in fact, with a desire for consistent philosophical conceptions to serve as a support for the laws and phenomena, and to embrace in one whole all that such sciences make known. Yet within the last century there has been an increasing inclination to direct minds more and more exclusively to phenomena, and philosophy (especially in this country) has been more and more discredited and neglected, till the very name "metaphysics" has become a bye-word of reproach. As might have been expected, however, a reaction has set in, and for the last five and twenty years the importance of philosophy and its actual necessity as a basis for science has been more and more obtaining recognition, and the reaction is well exemplified by the declarations of our most esteemed teachers of natural science. On the continent the same spectacle meets our view, and Strauss, Büchner, Vogt, and Hartmann aid powerfully, even by their destructive efforts, in directing popular attention to fundamental questions of philosophy which underlie all physical science.

There can be little doubt but that the further advance of science must aid indirectly in furthering that philosophic evolution which has next to occupy us. Nay, it is probable that the great philosophic reaction, towards which we seem to be rapidly approaching, would not be possible did not physical science attain a great development and wide popularity—so many minds being driven into philosophy through science. Thus through the science of matter, an increasing number of thinkers will come to have their attention directed to the science of mind. Recognising that "the proper study of mankind is man," and the all-importance of the old Delphic Γνῶθι σεαυτόν, they will necessarily be led to "psychology" (the portal of "metaphysics"), and thence to those questions which have occupied the noblest minds in all ages.

But leaving for the present the question of philosophy, let us seek the best answer we can get to our special question here—the effect of scientific evolution on the Church and her ministers.

We have seen that physical science must go on increasing and diffusing itself while the disconnection of the clergy from the pursuit and attainment of distinction in the field of such science is likely to widen. At the same time we have seen that the assertions of Christian theology are not of a nature to be capable of disproof by any science of the kind. If physics could demonstrate that there is no knowable or personal First Cause; that no prototypal design in eternity preceded the orderly evolution of the physical universe in time; if it could show that death, which necessitates the cessation of intellectual action as we experience it, necessarily or certainly renders all intellectual action impossible; if it could demonstrate that Christ never lived or never rose, the blessed Virgin was not immaculately conceived, or that there is no Divine presence in the eucharist,—then indeed the triumph of such science would but be another phrase to denote the annihilation of Christianity; but to all such questions physical science can have necessarily nothing to say. But it is here contended, not only that the growth of physical science cannot in itself have an ultimately detrimental effect on the Church, but that its very growth is accidentally calculated to indirectly bring about results of an opposite character. If when we come to consider philosophic evolution, we find reason to believe that such evolution will not be prejudicial to Christianity, then the number of Christians (and of the adherents of that natural religion of reason which Christianity takes for its basis) must continue to be large. In that case both its teachers and disciples must come to share in, and be more or less thoroughly imbued with, that physical science culture which it has been supposed will hereafter be so generally diffused. They will thus be guarded from simply accepting—as so many (through ignorance) now accept—the dogmatic assertions of some physical experts that a real incompatibility exists between science and religion. Also, many adherents of natural theology will as surely become convinced that arguments which they have discovered to be futile as directed against natural religion have neither more nor less weight as directed against Christianity.* On the other hand, the very arguments

---

* The late Mr. John Stuart Mill in his " Autobiography " (p. 70) laments that " those who reject revelation very generally take refuge in an optimistic deism, a worship of the order of nature and the supposed course of providence, *at least* as full of contradictions and perverting to the moral sentiments as any of the forms of Christianity, if only it is completely realised." At pp. 38, 39, he tells us that his father held Butler's "Analogy" in esteem, and that it "kept him, as he said, for some considerable time, a believer in the divine authority of Christianity, by proving to him that whatever

which they have to adduce in favour of natural theology
will by many be seen to apply further, and plainly
serve as supports to the foundations of Christianity while
harmonising with its whole genius and structure.

Again, physical science being almost universally diffused, will have lost its aspect of novelty, and also
"aggressiveness" will be clearly seen to be no proper
attribute of science, but only of certain definite philosophical systems previously associated with it.

The laity will not find many amongst their clergy
distinguished in physical science; but this result will not
be altogether unwelcome to them, because, however proper
they may deem it for priests, under peculiar social conditions, or now and again through some special vocation,
to devote themselves to physical science, yet they must
abstractedly consider " Pegasus harnessed to the plough,"
as a symbol quite inadequate to represent the incongruity
between such an employment and the ecclesiastical state.

---

are the difficulties in believing that the Old and New Testaments
proceed from, or record the acts of, a perfectly wise and good Being,
the same and still greater difficulties stand in the way of the belief
that a Being of such a character can have been the maker of the
universe. He considered Butler's argument as conclusive against
the only opponents for whom it was intended. Those who admit an
omnipotent as well as perfectly just and benevolent maker and ruler
of such a world as this, *can say little against Christianity, but what
can, with at least equal force, be retorted against themselves*"! On
this subject consult the *Dublin Review* for January, 1874, Art. I..
" Mr. Mill's Philosophical Position."

Yet though they will not find their clergy distinguished, they will find them universally as well acquainted with physical science as will be the bulk of cultivated men not specially devoted to it. They will thus be naturally encouraged to an increased confidence and trust in their religious teachers, whilst the latter will *demonstrate* to the laity (by the mere fact of the mode of life they have chosen, for all their physically scientific culture) the really neutral character of all physical science in its relations with religion. Finally the clergy, having been compelled by circumstances to make this closer acquaintance with physical science, will know and be able to point out readily and exactly what they may deem to have been the inferential errors of the preceding period as well as to combat more effectively such venerable conservatives as may continue to reiterate arguments analogous to some of the dysteleological * arguments of to-day.

If the foregoing views are correct, it seems to follow that, together with the changes anticipated, the Church's ministers may not improbably regain much of that social and political influence which they have at present lost. Not that such influence will be exercised directly, as was the case in the Middle Ages—the process of division of

---

* Dysteleology is a term which Professor Haeckel has devised to denote the study of the "*purposelessness*" of organs. An argument founded on such a conception, and relating to the *appendix vermiformis*, has already been noticed.

labour alone would render that impossible. Their influence will only be able to be exercised indirectly by the peaceful process of persuading public opinion.

Thus it appears to the writer of this essay that the process of scientific evolution, and the action of the actively anti-Christian section of the community will probably result in the development of a clergy and laity more thoroughly, because more reflectively and self-consciously, Christian and scientific in their physio-philosophical views than the world has yet seen. Some of the most recent developments in physiology, notably that of the nervous centres, and the most modern discoveries in anthropology, are, to say the least, singularly harmonious with the Church's traditional teaching. Such developments and such discoveries may be, and probably are, fatal to crude views popularly considered religious and Christian in this country such, *e.g.*, *as reciprocal action* of soul and body, and the existence of a primitive civilisation, in the vulgar acceptation of that phrase. But they harmonise perfectly with the traditional teaching of theologians concerning the *anima forma corporis,* and *homo sylvaticus,* and with principles laid down centuries before such discoveries were made. Few religious controversial errors are more common than that of supposing that a Christian doctrine has been refuted, when in fact it is but a post-Cartesian superstition that has been laid low, and thereby the old traditional view has become the more strengthened and justified. Descartes forsook the old traditional teaching as to the soul for speculative novelties of his own, which have spread far and wide, with the natural result of disgusting scientific physiologists with views erroneously supposed to be specially orthodox. Here, however, we are approaching the philosophical domain.

To conclude, there appears much reason for supposing that the process we have attempted to follow will be the occasion indeed for the abandonment of Christianity by many individuals, but that nevertheless the Church herself will be strengthened and made, not only more capable of self-defence on the scientific arena, but also more vigorous and better armed for attack against adversaries who now possess very great influence. We have here, in fact, another aspect of the same process referred to in "political evolution"—that which renders bracing climates, rough living, and absence of medical aid, beneficial to a "community," however fatal to "individuals," by killing off weak members and reducing it to a compact community of hardy and vigorous survivors.

The doctrines of the Church, whether they are or are not founded on fact, will at least receive an unexpected and powerful support and justification, if it comes to be demonstrated with regard to fresh scientific theories hereafter (as it has already been with evolution), that they are powerless weapons as employed against her, she having asserted beforehand principles amply sufficient to shield her from such attacks. As to evolution as applied to animal life, it is absolutely unquestionable by any one who understands the meaning of the terms that "it is evident that ancient and most venerable theological authorities distinctly assert *derivative* creation, and thus their teaching harmonises with all that modern science can possibly require."* As the present writer has elsewhere observed : † "It can hardly be denied to be a noteworthy fact, that the Church should have unconsciously provided for the reception of modern theories by the omission of fruitful principles and far-reaching definitions centuries before such theories were promulgated, and when views directly contradicting them were held universally, and even by those very men themselves who laid down the principles and definitions referred to. Circumstances so remarkable, such undesigned coincidences, which, as *facts*, cannot be denied, must be allowed to have been 'preordained' by all those who, being theists, assert that a 'purpose' runs through the whole process of cosmical evolution. Such theists must admit that, however arising or with whatever end, a prescience has watched over the Church's definitions, and that she has been so *guided* in her teaching as to be able to harmonise and assimilate with her doctrines the most modern theories of physical science."

---

* "Genesis of Species," 2nd edition, p. 305.
† "Lessons from Nature," p. 449.

But the widespread reception of the doctrine of organic evolution aids Christianity in yet two other ways. In the first place, it aids it by making more clearly manifest than before to those who are neither theologians nor philosophers the extreme importance of the Christian dogma of creation, both by the fatal consequences erroneously deduced from evolution by those who believe its affirmation to be equivalent to the denial of creation, and by the enthusiastic reception given to evolution by Darwin, Huxley, Haeckel, and others, expressly on the very ground of the supposed refutation by it of that cardinal Christian doctrine. Secondly, it aids Christianity by demonstrating how hopeless is the impossibility of refuting that dogma by any advance of physical science; for the most hostile efforts of the most skilled assailants have to their despite resulted in the decorating and filling in as it were, of the Christian doctrine of creation, instead of ending in its hoped for overthrow. For, as will be urged in the next chapter, the congruity of creative action with the universe, as manifested in our own free will, is made plain to us on *à priori* grounds; and, similarly, from a consideration of the nature of the First Cause, we are compelled to regard all existing forms, organic and inorganic, as responding to prototypal ideas in God.* With these conceptions once accepted, we

---

* See "Lessons from Nature," pp. 275 and 279.

can now see, on evolutionary principles, how in the instantaneous creation taught by St. Augustine the whole vast series of animal and vegetable forms, created potentially "in the beginning," have become actual from time to time as the conditions for their manifestation have in their appointed order from time to time occurred. Indeed, even the literal narrative of Scripture as to creation must be acknowledged to have been a remarkable anticipation of modern views compared with other ancient cosmogonies. This is confessed even by Haeckel, who speaks of it as distinguished "by the simple and natural chain of ideas which runs through it, and which contrasts favourably with the confused mythology of creation current among most of the other ancient nations;" there, he adds, "two great and fundamental ideas meet us . . . with surprising clearness and simplicity,—the idea of separation or *differentiation*, and the idea of progressive development or *perfecting*." Whatever divergence of opinion, however, may exist as to the sense and meaning of the words of Genesis, any disproof of the Christian doctrine authoritatively taught by St. Augustine is absolutely impossible.

There seems then to be nothing in the process of scientific evolution to cause reasonable alarm and anxiety to Christians, or to afford their opponents any well-grounded hope. Such evolution can indeed be indirectly influential through the philosophy which may be mixed up with it, but by that alone. The question then as to the future course of the philosophic aspect of contemporary evolution is the supremely important question of all those connected with that great modern movement, the Renaissance, made up as it is of the partly allied partly conflicting elements of paganism and civicism. To this question the writer proposes to next address himself.

CHAPTER V.

PHILOSOPHIC EVOLUTION.

THE attempt has been made in the last chapter to trace the effect on Christianity of a further evolution of physical knowledge, and the conclusion arrived at was that such evolution must be itself comparatively uninfluential, inasmuch as it could act only indirectly by stimulating the diffusion of philosophical ideas. In the third chapter we saw reason to believe that the results of political evolution would also depend upon the course hereafter taken by philosophy. We have here, then, to consider that supreme question concerning the result of the Renaissance movement, namely, the philosophical direction it is likely to take, with the hope of being able to form a final judgment as to the result of the great conflict between reviving paganism and the Christian Church.

The prospect that first strikes the eye of one surveying the field of contemporary speculative activity cannot be very encouraging to the lover of Christianity. Strauss, Büchner, Vogt, Haeckel, and Hartmann in Germany at present attract the sympathies of multitudes now co-operating, at least in will, with the attack made by Bismarck at the same time on both freedom and Christianity. In France, though the school of Comte is comparatively small, yet English sensationalism, that of Mr. Spencer, is making considerable advances, while the old Voltairian spirit holds its own with a tenacity similar to that possessed by the "principles of 1789." In Italy the English and German speculative schools are also making inroads, while, if such is not yet the case in the Iberian Peninsula, traditional convictions are gradually losing their hold, so that such exemption may perhaps be mainly assigned to political conditions unfavourable for intellectual activity.

In England a remarkable change has come over the spirit of the nation, and now by a singular coincidence even the liveliest sentiments of pity for the brute creation happen to concur with popular science in tending to obscure the distinction between rational and irrational natures, and in promoting a ready acceptance of the great doctrine concerning the essential bestiality of man. This doctrine is here specially referred to because it has in fact become the test doctrine by which the philosophical position of teachers and disciples may best be gauged.* In the fourth chapter of this essay it was stated that a certain philosophy was much diffused by means

---

* Mr. A. J. Mott, in his opening address, October, 1873, to the Literary and Philosophical Society of Liverpool, p. 3, says: "Questions concerning the origin of mankind have become either the radiating or the culminating points in most branches of science."

of physically scientific teaching, a strongly anti-Christian philosophic school, of which Strauss may be taken as a type, having eagerly caught at such physical teaching as a most convenient auxiliary.

The English of the eighteenth century were the leaders in speculative thought, and for all the great praise often bestowed upon German culture, the same may be said of those of our metaphysical writers of to-day who also deal with physical science. Darwin has nowhere so great a following as in Germany, while Mill has no slight influence in the land where his ashes repose. It will, it is believed, then, be amply sufficient for our purpose if we mainly direct our attention to the English sensational school which is ousting Hegel in Germany, and Cousin in France, and which claims to have done justice to Kant and Reid by harmonising the truths they held with the apparently contradictory, but really complementary, verities put forward by those they refuted. The teaching of the English school, as represented, amongst others, by Mill, Bain, Spencer, and Lewes, logically culminates in three negations; namely, of God, the soul, and virtue. Yet this is the school still honoured by the University of London with its exclusive patronage, thus imbuing with its doctrines the minds of all our most cultured youth. If such a system can sustain itself, and, still more, if it can propagate itself, its effect on Christianity need not be stated. These terms, which some may be disposed to think too severe as applied to our popular English system, cannot be fully justified here. It must suffice to remind readers that by Professor Clifford atheism is now avowed, that Spencer declares theism to be not even thinkable, and that the subordinate systems of all the school necessarily deny virtue in refusing every element of spontaneity to the human will. But this denial is not less evident from yet another point of view. According to the popularly received view of evolution—the view that is put forward by Spencer, Darwin, Bastian, Vogt, Büchner, and Haeckel—virtue is absolutely identified with the most brutal selfishness. As Mr. Martineau has tersely put it:* " Conscience is a hoarded fund of traditionary pressures of utility; . . . our highest attributes are only the lower that have lost their memory, and mistake themselves for something else." Two considerations, however, present themselves at once with reassuring aspect to the student of the various systems just now in vogue. These are, first, their discord and the internecine war amongst the teachers of these various systems, and secondly, the grotesqueness of the idol which each severally offers to the homage of his followers. Thus Mr. Mill and Mr. Spencer diverge respecting even the very foundation of the whole fabric of knowledge, which foundation the second asserts, while the first denies, to be "incon-

* *Contemporary Review*, April, 1872, p. 610.

ceivability." Mr. Bain and Mr. Spencer also differ on the same question; Mr. Bain asserting "experience," and not "inconceivability," to be the basis of certitude. The "principle of contradiction" presents another point on which they differ. Comte's teaching is repudiated with apparent scorn by Mr. Spencer, while quite lately a wide divergence* from the teaching of the last-named writer has been introduced by his brother sensist, Mr. G. H. Lewes, no less than from that of Mr. Mill.†

In this their mutual destructiveness the negative philosophers of our day but follow in the footsteps of their predecessors of the last three centuries; and were it not that "while the grass grows the steed starves," and that we need something positive, such systems might be left unassailed to the action of their own mutually disintegrating influences.

The curious objects presented to veneration by these systems may claim a passing notice.

We have first the "Unknowable"‡ as an object whereon

---

* Thus, in his "Problems of Life and Mind," Mr. Lewes describes "conceptions" as "symbols" (p. 191), and affirms that the "object felt exists precisely as it is felt" (p. 192). Again (p. 420) he says that what is "unpicturable" may be "conceivable," and he plainly declares his dissent from Mr. Spencer's "transfigured realism."

† As when Mr. Lewes asserts (p. 398) that the truths respecting triangles are not generalisations but intuitions, and again (p. 424), when he declares that "much" that Mill includes under induction is either "intuition" or "description."

‡ It is rather amusing to find how much is after all "known"

to expend our religious instincts, an entity without intelligence or volition, without an affection or a purpose, as much the cause of everything vile as of all we most admire—an entity to be saluted only by exclamations (vocal or mental) of "It is! It is!"

Then we have the "universum" of Strauss, the contempt of Schopenhauer for which was so great a sin in the eyes of the former, seeing that Strauss demanded for his idol (what from no sane man will he ever get) a devotion such as a good man feels for his God!

A more naturally popular, but really as absurd an idol is that "humanity" of M. Comte, so curtly dismissed by Mr. Spencer* as a quite inadequate object of reverence, which a little reflection readily enough shows it to be. Small value can ever be widely set on the "immortality" which positivism promises to its faithful disciples, and for the following reasons: 1. Few persons will care for a popularity which follows upon their utter personal annihilation. 2. Few, again, can hope for such immortality at all, since the immense majority of men must be content to die unknown. 3. Still fewer, it may be affirmed, would really prize posthumous veneration by

---

about this "Unknowable." Thus we learn from Professor Tyndall ("Use and Limit of the Imagination in Science") that it is known to have what may be compared with "shores," and further than these "shores of the unknowable" are *known* to be "infinite."

* "Study of Sociology," p. 311.

public opinion, when they consider how many really contemptible and vile characters have been popularly revered. 4. The positivist heaven is, moreover, necessarily denied to many of the most virtuous, since it is a necessary condition of the virtue of many to live obscure and unknown. 5. Finally, the difficulty which a conscientious man experiences in estimating even *his own* motives and character, shows how simply impossible it is for many men accurately and justly to estimate each other's real merits. But one of the drollest notions of what may fitly inspire reverence is put forth by Mr. Spencer himself; not indeed in his own person, but in that of an imaginary disputant, whose discourse he calls "comparatively consistent." This disputant is made to speak* of the oscillations of molecular motion thus: "The activities of this imponderable substance, though far simpler, and in that respect far lower, than the activities we call mind, are at the same time far *higher* than those we call mind in respect of their *intensity*, their velocity, their subtlety. . . . Thought is quick, light is many millions of times quicker." Thus quick and strong jumpings and very complex antics are relatively "*high*"—using that word in the sense we *apply it to mind*. Exceedingly complex gyrations of atoms are thus higher than "love of God or man." Contemplating in imagination the atomic oscillations which this view of

---

* "Psychology," vol. i., p. 622.

the universe puts before him, the Spencerian disciple may be imagined to exclaim: What wonderfully oscillating atoms! how noble! with what energy and rapidity do they not vibrate! they are divine! *Venite, adoremus!* As has been said, Mr. Spencer has not adopted this view as his own answer to an imaginary objector; nevertheless he patronises it as a "comparatively consistent" one, and certainly does not condemn it as nonsense; yet it is really wonderful how any one man of intelligence should for a moment imagine that any other could think material particles to be one bit more "noble" compared with "mind," let them perform what gyrations they may, or that they were made even a trifle "higher" by such restlessness. This passage reminds us of the Emersonian religion latent in the pious pirouettes of Fanny Ellsler.* Returning to our main subject, we may note yet another curious phenomenon. We refer to the strange contradiction presented by the Sensist school, which contains reasoners who ignore reason, and teachers of others, who not content with ignoring their own *ego* as a substance, fail to appreciate their own passing logical activity. Mr. Spencer and Mr. Lewes, however fundamentally they differ, agree in representing "inference" as really nothing but "association." No doubt the *sense-judgment*, so to speak, of brutes, is the imagination of unapparent

---

* See *Contemporary Review*, January, 1872, p. 187; and "Lessons from Nature," p. 362.

sensibles through association with felt sensibles; but *rational-judgment* is, at the least, the taking up and transformation of this sensible association by the action of a self-conscious intellect. Mr. Lewes* speaks of bees feeling geometry in constructing their cells. They feel, of course; but to imply they have thereby any appreciation of geometry would be hardly less unreasonable than to imply the same of crystallising salt or sugar. The "logic" of sense is truly "logic," but it is the logic of some one else, not of the brute that feels. Mr. Lewes, however, makes a remark of so strange a character, that it is impossible after reading it not to hesitate before accepting any opinion of his respecting intellect. Speaking † of "instinct" as being, according to his strange notion, "lapsed or indiscursive intelligence," he says: "The objection will doubtless be raised that instinct is wholly destitute of the characteristic of intelligence in that it has no choice: its operation is fixed, fatal. The reply is twofold: in the first place, the objection, so far as it has validity, applies equally to judgment where, given the premisses, the conclusion is fatal, no alternative being open. Axioms, in this sense, are logical instincts. Thus the highest intellectual process is on a level with this process said to be its opposite." "On a level!"—"applies equally!" Why, here the essential distinction

---

* "Problems of Life and Mind," p. 240.
† Op. cit., p. 141.

between "instinct" and "reason" is utterly ignored. "Instinct" is "fatal," but *blind.* Reason is "fatal," but *sees.* Axioms cannot be "instincts," because they are *seen* to be true, and are not blindly followed.

But is it possible for modern philosophy to culminate in such unsatisfactory and misleading exhibitions as this? It may be safely affirmed that self-contradiction, confusion, and that speculative annihilation, philosophical scepticism, must be the logical outcome of all such modern philosophy as either ignores the distinctive characters of reason, or denies our certainty of our own continued substantial existence, as does the philosophy alike of Mill, of Huxley, and of Spencer. The limits of this essay prohibit any attempt to demonstrate the latter operation; and it is the less necessary as the present writer has endeavoured elsewhere * to make it clear. But it may be here remarked, first, that it is logically impossible to deny our knowledge of the substantial and persisting *ego* without at the same time implying such knowledge; and secondly, that uncertainty on the matter can alone be justified by introducing a scepticism so complete that the doubt itself vanishes in the uncertainty which follows as to whether such doubt is not after all, certainty, ending in mental paralysis and the breakdown of all possible philosophy. But, once more, is this and

---

* See " Lessons from Nature," chap. i.

such as this the end of modern philosophic evolution? As the New Academy has seemed to some to close the cycle of Greek speculative thought, is a hopeless and absolute philosophic scepticism to close that of the modern period? That such is to be the end, Comte, as all know, has broadly proclaimed, and his English sympathiser, Mr. G. H. Lewes, for all his verbal changes about "metaphysics" and "metempirics," is as persistent as ever in denying the possibility of solving all those problems which have ever occupied the minds of the highest intellects; which problems he collectively stigmatises as "metempirical."

So gloomy and despairing a view is by no means shared by the present writer; on the contrary, he looks forward with confident hope to great metaphysical progress at no very distant period, and he sees no cause of discouragement in a certain apparent barrenness of results attending recent speculation. Progress is not uniform, but is effected by successively advancing waves, and even thus very unequally—advance in some directions being generally accompanied by, at least temporary, retrogression in others.

The artistic triumphs of Greece were not attained without an accompanying ethical depression, and when the decaying Græco-Roman civilisation became largely replaced by that of hardy Teutons, fresh from the baptismal font, barbarian art accompanied the moral renovation. The literary culture of the Renaissance was synchronous with a wide-spread loss of political liberty to the profit of centralised despotism, while the gradual growth and consolidation of our parliamentary system marks a period of continued architectural decline. Mr. Lecky has, in his "History of Rationalism," admirably demonstrated to us how widespread sentiments and habits of thought simply drop out of fashion, and how beliefs which have never been disproved, and with their evidence still unrefuted, come gradually to be abandoned and their evidence ignored, till a quite contradictory belief is eventually accepted. A wave of sentiment, far more than any logical process, repelled from men's minds the doctrine of man's ape origin when it was first mooted. It is the flow of an opposite wave of sentiment which determines its wide-spread acceptance now. Might we not then expect, *à priori*, that the great advance in natural knowledge of the last three centuries—those marvellous discoveries which have more and more directed men's minds to physical observation and experiment—should be accompanied by stagnation or retrogression along some other lines of thought?

Attention cannot fully be directed to two distinct inquiries simultaneously, and an exhausting pursuit of physics must necessarily starve some other intellectual habit. We should then be little surprised to find for a time a philosophical decline accompanying scientific advance. Moreover, it is ever the wont of men's minds to depreciate the object of admiration of the period immediately preceding. We can view with more or less admiration the costume of a century past, but the fashion of some five or ten years ago seems to us more or less absurd, as well as distasteful. Thus each past activity has to wait for its due appreciation, until the period of unjust depreciation which has followed it has passed by.

The architectural glories of Northern Europe, those mediæval structures, at once (from their beauty and true principles of construction) poems and scientific treatises in stone, have only of late years ceased to be despised as barbarous. Now, universally appreciated, fragments of ruins which happy accident has saved from destruction, are guarded with jealous care, and thoughtfully studied as revelations of a skill and refinement which have passed from amongst us.

As it is now with the material constructions of the Middle Ages, so, we may find reason to think, will it be to a yet greater extent with the far more marvellous intellectual fabrics those ages have bequeathed us. The soaring lightness of such lofty arches as those of the choir of Le Mans awake our admiration by reason of their beauty; but our wonder is yet more exercised by the solidity of those slender piers and towering buttresses, which, arch over arch, hold securely poised so vast a roof of stone at such an airy height. Similarly, the wonderful acuteness, the delicacy and subtlety of distinction to be found in Scholastic writers are already exciting the wonder of the few who, following the example of Sir William Hamilton, are beginning to make acquaintance with them. But it may be that wonder will ere long be much more widely excited by the solidity of the reasoning those acute and delicate minds thought out. A foretaste of such appreciation with respect to the philosophy of this period has lately been given us by one of its most distinguished opponents. The Lord Rector of Aberdeen, addressing his subjects thought it well to tell them :—*

"The Scholastic philosophy is a wonderful monument of the patience and ingenuity with which the human mind tried to build up a logically consistent theory of the universe. . . . And that philosophy is by no means dead and buried, as many vainly suppose. On the contrary, numbers of men of no mean learning and accomplishment, and sometimes of rare power and subtlety of thought, hold by it as the best theory of things which has yet been stated. And, what is more remarkable, men who speak the language of modern philosophy nevertheless think the thoughts of the Schoolmen."

It may be well, perhaps, now to state the reasons which make this increased appreciation probable.

Mr. Spencer has remarked: "During all past times

---

* See *Contemporary Review*, March, 1874, p. 667.

mankind have eventually gone right, after trying all possible ways of going wrong." * The same course mankind appears also to follow in philosophic speculation. The great process of *reductio ad absurdum* has attended the evolution of our post-mediæval metaphysics; the logical result is scepticism. The intellectual paralysis (as respects philosophy) attending the modern sensational school, which is essentially the school of Hume, has already been noted; it remains to call attention to the fact that Hume's philosophy is the logical consequence of the metaphysics referred to. That such is the case, indeed, the event has shown. Berkeley's mind was far too acute not to build logically on the premisses he accepted from Locke, and the same may be said of Hume with respect to Berkeley. The refutation which Kant for a time effected has been itself refuted by the aid of that very evolutionary process which Kant himself favoured and foreshadowed. In spite of the efforts of the philosopher of Königsberg, in spite of Reid and his followers in England, and of Royer-Collard, Maine-de-Biran, Jouffroy, and Cousin in France, the most extreme sensationalism is once more in possession of the field, ranging from Naples to Aberdeen, and from Bordeaux to St. Petersburgh.

Thus the teaching of the whole school of modern meta-

---

* "Study of Sociology," p. 306.

physics ends in scepticism, in nihilism, as the ultimate result of materialism and idealism.

It will naturally be asked, then, If such is not to be the end of philosophic evolution, what is the remedy, and how is recuperative force to be obtained?

The reply here offered is, that a remedy is to be obtained by digging deeper. No mere return to Kant is adequate to meet a scepticism which so much of Kant's system completely justifies. It is impossible to secure to practical reason its objective validity, if "pure" reason be declared fallacious. If the view here advocated be correct, what is needed, and what evolution will infallibly bring about, is not a return to *a* philosophy, but a return to *the* philosophy. For if metaphysics are possible, there is not, and never was or will be, more than one philosophy which, properly understood, unites all speculative truths and eliminates all errors: *the* philosophy of *the* philosopher—Aristotle.

But, it will be exclaimed,—This is throwing us into confusion; all the speculative discussions of the last two thousand years and more will have to be gone through again! Aristotle is understood in many senses, and has given rise to many schools. It would be hardly less irrational to refer us to the Bible for theology than to refer us to Aristotle for philosophy! And the propriety of the objection would be conceded, did there not exist a continuous traditional line of philosophic evolution, bringing down the peripatetic philosophy to the present day. Others may exclaim, this is stagnation, or even reaction. But there is of course no real danger of either; the laws of evolution in general render it absurd to suppose that stagnation, or a really reactionary reversal of development, can ever be possible. All that is possible is that speculation may revert to a temporarily abandoned line of inquiry, experience having demonstrated that all other possible lines end blindly.

Many persons may be surprised to read the assertion that such a continuous and traditional school of philosophy exists at all; but that it does exist is none the less a truth. The peripatetic philosophy simply fell out of fashion at the period of the Renaissance, when in the scientific and literary intoxication of the period, with its reviving Platonism, pantheism, and paganism, men left traditional lines of speculative thought to fall into bondage to the philosophical empiric Descartes and the wonderfully over-estimated Bacon. The French philosophical heresiarch—the logical father both of our modern materialists and idealists—never understood—he had never even learned—the philosophy he ignorantly opposed. That philosophy, ridiculed and overborne, but never refuted, was pushed aside by the force of the popular current, and became, after a time, like the architecture of the colleges it had illustrated, a byeword of reproach and contempt; till, ignored and forgotten, the world is astonished to learn that it has never ceased to have both teachers and disciples. It is even amusing to observe how pointless are many of the arguments of moderns such as Mr. Spencer, Mr. Lewes, etc., from their want of acquaintance with the Scholastics, and the simple way* in which they think that all is done when Kant has been replied to, and that it is quite needless to go further back.

Some readers may be disposed to ask, Where has this philosophy been preserved, and who are its teachers now?

At the epoch of that flood of barbarian invasion which overspread a world deemed by so many to be approaching its end, the treasures of classic literature found fortunate shelter within the libraries of Benedictine monasteries, scattered far and wide in dense forests, savage, rocky solitudes, or dismal swamps. Those black-robed monks, whose manual labour spread agriculture over Northern Europe, not content with ministering to the peoples' bodily and spiritual needs, paved the way for refined

---

* Thus Mr. Spencer ignores all philosophy anterior to Descartes, and contents himself with Berkeley, Hume, and Kant, as examples of the moderns. Mr. Lewes (" Problems," vol. i., p. 437) actually affirms, "All modern metempirics are either Kantian or founded upon Kantian principles." For examples of complete misapprehension of the only philosophy worthy the name, and consequently futile argumentation, see pp. 152, 212, 214, 245, 249, 265, 271, 278, 363, 368, 437, and 447.

mental culture by their preservation of so many writings which, but for them, would have been finally lost to us. For these deeds the gratitude of all enlightened men of all creeds or of none has been and is theirs; and thus when modern vandalism recently threatened with destruction the venerable abbey of Monte Cassino, some of our noblest fellow-countrymen allowed no difference of belief to hinder their energetic protest against so cruel a blow to history, to literature, and to the glory of the Italian nation itself.

At the epoch of that flood of pagan intoxication which overspread Europe at the Renaissance, as the culture of the traditional philosophy passed from disesteem to abandonment, it found a fortunate shelter also within religious houses, and especially (as was most natural) with the Dominicans. The mission of the friar-preachers was, however (for some centuries to come at least), mainly accomplished, and thus we have to look elsewhere for its most efficient support. Just at the critical moment there appeared in the arena of speculative conflict those ever fresh spiritual athletes, the sons of St. Ignatius of Loyola. In their colleges the traditional philosophy has been scrupulously preserved, and from Suarez and Lugo to Kleutgen (now living in exile) an uninterrupted body of teachers has carried on its cultivation and development, applying its principles again and again in opposition to the various errors as they have arisen, from the time of the society's foundation to the present day. As gratitude is now due, and widely acknowledged, to the Benedictines, for their preservation during the illiterate ages of our choicest literary treasures, so gratitude is now due, and will one day be even more widely acknowledged, to the Jesuits for their preservation during the whole Renaissance movement of our choicest philosophic treasures, as main guardians of the peripatetic tradition.

The fathers of the society enjoy the glory of perennial persecution and hostility; and, whatever may be the view taken of their merits, and whatever good men may oppose them, all must admit that they at least possess the distinction conferred on them by the special hostility of all the vilest of mankind. Nevertheless, it is not impossible that their careful preservation for us of the traditional philosophy may one day be reckoned a yet greater distinction.

This philosophy then lives, and is taught amongst us here in England now, and it is to be regretted that some prominent English sensists do not profit by such teaching. Were one of the leaders of the modern school to cease altogether to write or teach for a period of some three years, and to endeavour to obtain for that period the hospitality of a Jesuit seminary, and there devote himself (merely *at first* as a learner, and not as a critic) to the acquisition of the peripatetic philosophy, his labour would not be lost. The present writer has too strong a belief in human free will to be confident that the supposed student's views would be thereby, as a matter of course, fundamentally modified, but is quite certain that his power and depth as a philosopher would be very greatly augmented, and, irrelevant matters being removed, controversy would be brought more aptly to an issue.

It may be asked, however, Wherein do you see actual signs of such a revival of philosophy? It may be answered, that amongst other indications the writer has positive information of the advance of the peripatetic philosophy in Germany; that Professor Ueberweg himself bore witness to such a movement; that Mr. Spencer's own writings tend to force it on; that Mr. Lewes' last book* is calculated to drive it forward at an accelerated rate; that its course is facilitated by the philosophy of Hart-

---

* See his "Problems of Life and Mind;" we find there good peripateticism as to the soul and body unconsciously set forth at pp. 112, 156, 160, and 161; as to the distinction between men and brutes, at pp. 124, 153-155, 157, 160, 169, 250, and 296; as to universals, at p. 136; as to the existence of "potential" knowledge, at p. 243; as to the sort of existence possessed by "co-ordination," "life," and "mind," at p. 281; as to terminology, at p. 336; as to the relation of the ideal to the real order, at p. 342; as to mathematical intuitions, at p. 398; as to the relations between imagination and conception, at p. 420. Even as to logic, as an art, he goes wrong rightly. Thus he says (p. 77), "There is no more an art of reasoning than there is an art of breathing or digesting." But peripatetic logic is an art in so far as it is

mann; and that the testimony of no less an opponent than Professor Huxley himself has borne witness to its vitality. Moreover, as will be almost immediately urged, recently discovered scientific facts and the direction of modern biological thought favour philosophical conceptions universally prevalent amongst men of culture four centuries ago, but which have since been generally neglected and ignored.

If, then, such a revival as is here indicated is indeed to be looked for; if that philosophy, in the terms of which the various Christian doctrines have been defined, is likely once more to play a prominent and dominant part in the intellectual world,—it is almost needless to point out that there can be no fear for Christianity. That evolution is taking such a course the present writer believes, and he consequently also believes that scientific and political evolution can but favour Christianity, in the modes predicted in former chapters of this essay, on the condition that philosophic evolution should be found to take no hostile direction. But if post-Cartesian philosophy has been so wanting in positive results, even from its own point of view, as is here maintained, are the gyrations it has gone through useless, and will the world be none the better for the expenditure of so much effort

cathartic, and that as we may improve our actual breathing or digestion through a knowledge of physiology, so we may practically improve our actual reasoning through a knowledge of the laws of thought.

and so much skill? Instead of such being the case, it seems probable that the post-Cartesian philosophy, of which Spencerism may be taken as the culmination, will have performed a most useful part. Indeed, considering how through it and its alliance with physical science, philosophy has penetrated where, but for these conditions, it might never have effected an entrance, it would be difficult to estimate its value and importance too highly. The main reason why the wide diffusion of Spencerism seems so advantageous is its bearing upon four fundamental objects :—I. The Ego. II. The Will. III. Nature. IV. God.

I. With respect to the Ego, the very pertinacity with which writers of the agnostic school (that of Huxley, Spencer, etc.) have denied that we know its existence with supreme certainty, and the very arguments which they have made use of to disprove such certainty have really aided, in no small degree, the cause they have sought to overthrow. They have so aided it, by making manifest the extreme importance of our knowledge of our own continued existence—the substantial Ego, and forcing on us a recognition explicitly of much that is implicitly contained and involved in that knowledge, but which is apt to be overlooked or neglected. For every one, who, by this controversy has, for the first time, brought home to him the really marvellous nature of his own present knowledge of his past states of being, will thereby be brought to recognise that he has a knowledge of absolute, objective truth. His eyes will thus be opened to the supremely important truth, that he is endowed with an intellect which is not shut up in a mere subjective knowledge of its own states and modifications, but which is endowed with the wonderful capacity of knowing absolute, objective truth external to these states. He will learn this through his recognition of the "veracity of memory," without accepting which he cannot advance one step in knowledge. Consciousness is of the present, but we cannot know our own continued existence without at the same time knowing the past. This consideration alone is sufficient to refute the whole experimental philosophy which teaches that we become nothing but phenomena. For "experience" itself is not possible, unless memory can be relied on as trustworthy. My "experience" would be of small value indeed, if I could not be absolutely certain that it was mine, and not that of some other person.*

Again, every one who recognises the truth of his knowledge of his own existence must equally recognise that his intellect declares certain dicta (such, *e.g.*, as that "what thinks exists," "the whole is greater than its part," "ingratitude is blameworthy") to be absolutely and universally true. He must further see, on examining the de-

---

* See "Lessons from Nature," p. 23.

clarations of his own intellect, that such truths as these are not agreed to by him out of sheer mental impotence—from mere inability to think the reverse—but that they are, on the contrary, truths which he apprehends actively, and which he sees to be positively necessary and absolutely universal, that they must be true in Sirius or the Pleiades, and that they were as true when the first film of mind laid the foundation of the Laurentian rocks. Thus again, his mind is in another mode carried by its own power and force out of the mere subjective and phenomenal into the objective and noumenal region of absolute external truth.

Once more, this self-knowledge will force on each one who investigates it, that his intellect has yet another power; namely, that proceeding by a peculiar logical process (ratiocination) to draw forth explicitly truths implicitly contained in other truths, but not fully apparent till so drawn forth. When to the proposition, "All the radii of one circle are equal," we add, "the lines A and B are radii of one circle," we see that a third truth is implicitly contained in these two propositions; which truth explicitly stated is the conclusion, "the lines A and B are equal," and the force of the whole process of influence is expressed by the word "*therefore*." This process forms yet another mode of arriving at real objective truth and knowledge other than phenomenal, for we learn that such lines as A and B must be equal everywhere and at all times, and that God Himself could not make them otherwise. The declarations of the intellect and its logical processes having been thus justified, its declarations as to "causation" and "morality" gain at once an unquestionable validity. It becomes a self-evident truth, that even if the material universe be eternal, its series of phenomenal, conditional changes, ranging in recurring cycles through a past eternity, must none the less require a real, absolute eternal Cause, while the absolute declarations of the intellect respecting morals will necessitate the attribution to that supreme Cause of "a goodness" harmonising with, however immeasurably exceeding, that of man. To put it shortly, this zealous propagation of the absurd denial of our knowledge of our own existence is but the prelude to a more thorough and complete understanding of that knowledge and of all which it involves, than any other cause (save such denial) could well be conceived as producing. In knowing our own continued existence, we come to know, with a supreme degree of certainty, a whole system of objective truths which the intellect is seen to have the wonderful power, not only of perceiving, but of perceiving to be objectively, absolutely, and universally true.

The facts here stated may be thus summed up :—

Our recognition of our own self-knowledge reveals to us objective truth and our possession of it.

It also shows us that there are universal, objectively necessary truths, and that we know them.

Also it causes us to recognise the validity of ratiocination, or the explicit evolution of implicit truth.

Hence we learn the validity of our inference as to the existence of a First Cause adequate to produce all that we know as existing in its effects, and therefore as necessarily possessing qualities, such that "intellect," "order," "purpose," etc., which we recognise as existing amongst its effects in ourselves, may be predicted of it in a superior degree; such human characteristics being but adumbrations of the corresponding qualities in such First Cause.

II. As to "Will." The persistency, and even passion, with which the declarations of the commonsense of mankind are met by denials that we possess even a fragment of really self-determining power, serve to make even clearer than before the marvellous and isolated character of the power of choice, as also the important truths which its assertion implies. When it comes to be fully appreciated by the many, how rigid law rules, not only all irrational living beings, as well as inanimate and inorganic creatures, but also even the vast majority of our own actions, the marvellous character of our power of voluntarily choosing the less attractive of two modes of action will be less inadequately estimated. It will become generally understood, that while we may be certain of possessing that power of choice which all unprejudiced men know that they possess, yet that in making a free act of choice they really dominate and control the whole chain of physical causation by their free will. As to the implications of this truth, it is evident that our own power of dominating physical causation renders supernatural action on the part of the First Cause not only credible, but to be anticipated *à priori*. Creative action, miracles, response to prayer, and the bestowal after death of rewards and punishments according to our exercise of volition during life, are not only completely congruous with a philosophy which asserts the freedom of the will, but are made antecedently probable by such philosophy. Indeed, that such is really the case may be judged from a consideration of who those are who deny our power of free volition. They are one and all opponents of religion, natural as well as revealed. It is daily becoming more and more apparent, that to deny free will is to deny even the existence—still more the obligation—of virtue, to uproot every possible basis of morality, and to eliminate from the social organism those legal sanctions, and even those modes of speech, which are bound up with the very existence of "rights" and "duties." Yet these men, finding themselves forced by inexorable logic to accept religion if they accept free will, prefer to deny it, in spite of all the above-mentioned consequences,—prefer to be untrue to the dicta of their own intellects as to necessary truths, and even to commit the absurdity of denying the supreme certainty to them of their own existence; more than this, they have every appearance of rejoicing in the doctrine of the bestiality of man, in the belief that they have no sentiment or aspiration which is not in root and essence the desire of food, or the brutal appetite of sex, or the dread of brutes more powerful or more malignant than themselves. This phenomenon is one of much interest, and very instructive. At first sight it seems almost incredible that such bitter hostility should exist. Yet, apart from religion, a certain explanation presents itself in the trial to pride which arises from the admission of free will, since it places the poorest peasant on an absolute equality, as to morality, with the most cultured and refined, since both are equally capable of exercising rational, meritorious volition. If there is such a thing as morality at all, it must necessarily be beyond comparison, as to value, with mental refinement, culture, or intellectual capacity; and it necessarily follows, that a rude savage, with no implements but a few chipped flints, may be above all comparison in nobility with the greatest of our agnostic philosophers, "while a poor, paralysed old woman, sitting in a chimney-corner, may, by her good aspirations and volitions, be repeatedly performing mental acts, compared with which the discovery by Newton of the law of gravitation is as nothing."*

Moreover, in free will and morality we have that which

---

* "Lessons from Nature," p. 380.

cannot be merely the result of the inheritance of the habitual actions, feelings, and imaginations of brutes. Conceptions of time and space may be with apparent plausibility (though not without real absurdity) represented as the results of structural modifications induced in a practically infinite brute ancestry, which had been ever submitted to conditions of time and space; but at any rate such ancestry was never at any time submitted to conditions of moral responsibility. It is in this way that the recognition of a power of choice in man, which only those false to their own reason can deny, renders the belief that man has been developed from a brute a true absurdity—a physical superstition which must vanish before the light spread abroad by a more diffused knowledge of the powers and declarations of the human intellect.

III. With respect to "nature," the modern conception of it is in many respects, as has been lately said, a return to older views, or at least harmonises with such. The prevailing views are indeed simply pantheistic, but all that is positive in such views may be easily assimilated with philosophic theism. Indeed, it may be affirmed that much in modern physiology demands the philosophy of Aristotle as its logical complement, and the doctrine of biological evolution needs pre-eminently the aid of the peripatetic doctrine of "matter" and "form."

Mr. Spencer's view of evolution itself may be taken

up and included within a larger one, which will then assume the part of "form" to the "matter" provided for us by Mr. Spencer.

Mr. Spencer's law is, that everything in the material universe is proceeding *from an indefinite, incoherent homogeneity to a definite, coherent heterogeneity*. But he supplies us with no explanatory basis for this law. We can see, by his system, neither its origin, its ultimate future, nor the principle of its continuity. Our philosophy, however, shows us (by means of our self-conscious substantial Ego, endowed with the power of knowing objective truth) a necessary First Cause—which amongst its attributes must have an intelligence and a will, such as find their faint and inadequate type in the corresponding faculties of the human soul. Such a Cause, as intelligent, cannot be self-contradictory, and hence necessarily follows the *continuity* of cosmical evolution. It must, as Will, have such an intensity of "purpose," that no human purpose can be comparable with it. "Hence necessarily follows *'final causality'*—the enchainment of all phenomena and their adaptation to ends in a heriarchy of augmenting activities, from celestial revolutions and the attractions and cohesions of sidereal masses, through vegetative life and animal sentiency up to self-consciousness and free volition; so that, from kingdom to kingdom, the creation may rise towards an ideal—by successively higher degrees of participation in the perfection of the First Cause itself."* By the union of these two laws of (1) continuity, and (2) final causality, the whole phenomena of the universe—physical, biological, political, moral, and religious—may be really explained and understood, and Mr. Spencer's law may be accepted as conveniently expressing its material aspect and mode of action. Whether or not the teleological part of this conception can be gathered from mere irrational nature directly, it can most certainly be obtained from a consideration of what is involved in our own self-consciousness. When such implication is brought thence and applied to the universe, nature, on a large scale and when broadly read, loudly confirms it, though, as might be expected, the application of the human mind to the task of thoroughly comprehending the purposes of God in any given phenomenon has led, as it must necessarily always lead, to delusion and disappointment.

The phenomena of cosmical evolution are presented by the Sensist school in terms of matter and force, and Mr. Spencer presents us with matter also reduced to conceptions of force. But that the universe can be explained by the conceptions of one sole force by itself, without any other force or any matter upon which such solitary force may act, is an evident absurdity. We must there-

---

* "Lessons from Nature," p. 358.

fore conceive at least two forces, or force and matter. But for a solitary force to act upon matter, that matter, even if consisting of but a single element, must have certain qualities and powers of response to incident forces —*i.e.*, we must conceive latent potentialities which incident forces may render actualities. " Hence we get the formal law of cosmical evolution—whereof Mr. Spencer's law is the material expression. This formal law may be defined as the continuous progress of the material universe by the unfolding of latent potentialities through the action of incident forces in harmony with a pre-ordained end, such unfolding exhibiting a change from indefinite incoherent homogeneity to definite coherent heterogeneity." *

It was before observed, that reason shows us that phenomenal changes, even if eternal, require an eternal absolute cause. It shows it us thus: The principle of causality teaches us that everything must be absolute or caused. Science reveals to us an indefinite series of passed phenomenal changes, but points to no beginning. Reason does not affirm that such changes may not have proceeded in cycles from all eternity, owing to an eternal collection of causal factors. If such collocation and factors be the absolute, we have pantheism, which is to be refuted by *à priori* demonstrations of reason as well as

---

* " Lessons from Nature," p. 361.

by the positive dicta of our intellect in the sphere of morality, revealing to us an absolute distinction between good and evil, which pantheism necessarily denies. If such collocation and factors be not the absolute, they are caused (that they are really fortuitous would probably be asserted by none of our modern school of philosophy, and this alternative may be neglected as absurd and obsolete). If such collocation and factors be caused, they cannot be caused by the whole sum of the phenomenal series, since this is the effect; still less by any part of it. They must, then, be caused by something external to the series and to the collocation of causal factors. " But if the phenomenal universe be eternal, this cause must be eternal. It must be absolute, as the cause of everything phenomenal and relative. It must be orderly and intelligent, as the cause of an orderly series of phenomena which reveals to us an objective intelligence in the bee and ant, not that of such animals themselves, but which harmonises with, and is recognised by, our own intellect."*
It must be adequate to produce all the phenomena which have been produced—amongst them power, intelligence, morality, and will; in other words, it must be God.

This Divine First Cause thus recognised by our intellect as necessarily existing, is more or less qualitatively revealed to us in the material universe according as we

---

* Op. cit., p. 358.

extend the sphere of our observations. It is concealed most completely when the inanimate creation is alone considered. It seems to assume a pantheistic form when we rise no higher than the brute creation. If man alone occupies our attention, a narrow anthropomorphic deism may be the result; but from a sympathetic study of the whole universe—the mineral, vegetable, animal, and human creations, including intellect, morality, and will,—the conception of Almighty God becomes fully revealed to the human intellect.

The process of evolution, as carried through the material world, shows us the evolution from potentiality into actuality of successively new forms. We cannot imagine how they are produced; we simply recognise that they are. In passing to the vegetable world from the mineral kingdom, we behold, for the first time manifested, a vital form. In passing to the animal world from the vegetable kingdom, we behold, for the first time manifested, a sentient form. In passing to the human world from the kingdom of brute animals, we behold, for the first time manifested, a rational form.

With our entrance on the world of self-conscious reason and free volition, we impinge upon another order of being from that revealed to us by all below it—an order of being which the cosmical universe, as it were, intersects, as the different lines of cleavage and stratification may intersect in the same rock.

The mingling of the hyperphysical world of rationality with the irrational creation is paralleled by the existence of crystals in plants, and by the action of the vegetable kingdom in modifying the results of merely physical and chemical laws.

Such mingling is again paralleled by the action of plants on animals and of animals on plants (as, *e.g.*, the necessity of insect-life for the fertilisation of many, and even for the nutrition of some plants), such fertilising action, perhaps, even occasioning important variations.

Modern science convincingly shows us that truth which St. Thomas taught centuries ago—that a successively increasing purpose runs through the irrational creation up to man. Cosmical entities and their laws *do* serve organic being more than inorganic, sentient being more than insentient, rational being more than sentient. Therefore, if the First Cause wills at all, He must have willed most service to man of all known creatures.

This increase of service (and consequent dependence) becomes manifest when we consider the following truths :

"The inorganic world can do without the organic, but not *vice versâ*. The vegetable world can exist without the animal, but not *vice versâ*. The animal world can do without the rational world as experienced by us, but not *vice versâ*. Therefore, if there is *intention* at all, all things are for man in the chief degree.

"The same law of progress extends through the evolution of human society. In politics, in law, in science, in art, and in religion,* we find the same law of evolution —continuity and final causality resulting in the manifestation of increasingly stable and definite varieties of being." †

IV. The last and supremely important result of modern philosophical controversies is the vividness with which they force on the many a higher appreciation of the awful, the inconceivable majesty of God, under the irrational term "the Unknowable." Certainly, however, nothing said on this subject by Mr. Spencer or by any other agnostic writer has not in effect been said over and over again by theologians of early, mediæval, and recent times. It is indeed amusing to read Mr. Spencer's objection to the application of the term "personality" to the First Cause as being inadequate, as if in so saying he had said anything new or important.

If he had only inquired, he would have found that every tyro in theology knows that not even "being" can be predicated univocally of God and creatures, while the special term *hyperhypostasis* is one familiar to theologians as denoting the supreme Personality, and is used to distinguish It from every subordinate and dependent personality. For all this, it cannot be denied

---

* See Dr. Newman's great work, "An Essay on the Development of Christian Doctrine."

† "Lessons from Nature," p. 360.

that grossly inadequate and absurdly anthropomorphic conceptions of God are far too common, while popular preachers or writers, by their inaccurate language, tend to spread yet farther such grossness and absurdity. Of course, after all, the difference between our highest conceptions of God and those of the rudest boor are as nothing compared with the difference between such highest conceptions and the Divine reality. Nevertheless, although our conceptions of God cannot be appreciably raised when viewed in relation to Him, yet in relation to ourselves they of course can be; and it is a very great gain to us to obtain and spread abroad in any way a somewhat higher and less inadequate notion of the being and nature of our Almighty Creator.

Now the controversy respecting "the Unknowable" must tend in this direction, and therefore really helps to promote that very theology which agnostics would fain abolish.

We may reasonably hope, with respect to many of these opponents of theology, that their opposition may be due rather to ignorance than to malice, and to want of acquaintance with the conception of God really entertained by Christian theologians. It may thus not be out of place to cite here the following passage, in which one of the most widely revered priests of our own country now living expresses the teaching of the Christian religion in this matter.

He tells us that:

"As in the human frame there is a living principle, acting upon it and through it by means of volition; so, behind the veil of the visible universe there is an invisible, intelligent Being, acting on and through it, as and when He will. This invisible Agent is in no sense a soul of the world, after the analogy of human nature; but, on the contrary, is absolutely distinct from the world, as being its Creator, Upholder, Governor, and Sovereign Lord. Here we are at once brought into the circle of doctrines which the idea of God embodies. I mean, then, by the Supreme Being, one who is simply self-dependent, and the only being who is such; moreover, that He is without beginning, or eternal, and the only eternal; that in consequence He has lived a whole eternity by Himself; and hence that He is all-sufficient for His own blessedness, and all blessed, and ever blessed. Further, I mean a Being who, having these prerogatives, has the supreme good, or rather is the supreme good, or has all the attributes of good in infinite greatness; all wisdom, all truth, all justice, all love, all holiness, all beautifulness; who is omnipotent, omniscient, omnipresent; ineffably one, absolutely perfect; and such, that what we do not know, and cannot even imagine of Him, is far more wonderful than what we do and can. I mean, one who is sovereign over His own will and actions, though always according to the eternal rule of right and wrong, which is Himself. I mean, moreover, that He created all things out of nothing, and preserves them every moment, and could destroy them as easily as He made them; and that, in consequence, He is separated from them by an abyss, and is incommunicable in all His attributes. And further, He has stamped upon all things, in the hour of their creation, their respective natures, and has given them their work and mission and their length of days, greater or less, in their appointed place. I mean, too, that He is ever present with His works, one by one, and confronts everything He has made by His particular and most loving Providence, and manifests Himself to each according to its needs; and on rational beings has imprinted the moral law, and given them power to obey it, imposing on them the duty of worship and service, searching and scanning them through and through with His omniscient eye, and putting before them a present trial and a judgment to come.

"Such is what theology teaches about God, a doctrine, as the very idea of its subject matter presupposes, so mysterious as in its fulness to lie beyond any system, and to seem even in parts to be irreconcilable with itself, the imagination being unable to embrace what the reason determines. It teaches of a Being infinite, yet personal; all blessed, yet ever operative; absolutely separate from the creature, yet in every part of the creation at every moment; above all things, yet under everything. It teaches of a Being who, though the highest, yet in the work of creation, conservation, government, retribution, makes Himself, as it were, the minister and servant of all; who, though inhabiting eternity, allows Himself to take an interest, and to feel a sympathy, in the matters of space and time. His are all beings, visible and invisible, the noblest and the vilest of them; His are the substance, and the operation, and the results of that system of physical nature into which we are born; His, too, are the powers and achievements of the intellectual essences, on which He has bestowed an independent action and the gift of organisation.

" The laws of the universe, the principles of truth, the relation of one thing to another, their qualities and virtues, the order and harmony of the whole, all that exists, is from Him; and, if evil is not from Him, as assuredly it is not, this is because evil has no substance of its own, but is only the defect, excess, perversion, or corruption of that which has. All we see, hear, and touch, the remote sidereal firmament, as well as our own sea and land, and the elements which compose them, and the ordinances they obey, are His. The primary atoms of matter, their properties, their mutual action, their disposition and collocation, electricity, magnetism, gravitation, light, and whatever other subtle principles or operations the wit of man is detecting or shall detect, are the works of His hands. From Him has been every movement which has convulsed and refashioned the surface of the earth.

"The most insignificant or unsightly insect is from Him, and good in its kind; the ever teeming, inexhaustible swarms of animalculæ, the myriads of living motes invisible to the naked eye, the restless, ever spreading vegetation which creeps like a garment over the whole earth, the lofty cedar, the umbrageous banana, are His. His are the tribes and families of birds and beasts, their graceful forms, their wild gestures, and their passionate cries. And so in the intellectual, moral, social, and political world. Man, with his motives and works, his languages, his propagation, his diffusion, is from Him. Agriculture, medicine, and the arts of life, are His gifts. Society, laws, government, He is their sanction. The pageant of earthly royalty has the semblance and the benediction of the Eternal King. Peace and civilisation, commerce and adventure, wars when just, conquest when humane and necessary, have His co-operation and His blessing upon them. The course of events, the revolution of empires, the rise and fall of states, the periods and eras, the progresses and the retrogressions of the world's history, not indeed the incidental sin, over abundant as it is, but the great outlines and the issues of human affairs, are from His dispositions. The elements and types and seminal principles and constructive powers of the moral world, in ruins though it be, are to be referred to Him. He 'enlighteneth every man that cometh into this world.' His are the dictates of the moral sense, and the retributive reproaches of conscience. To Him must be ascribed the rich endowments of the intellect, the radiation of genius, the imagination of the poet, the sagacity of the politician, the wisdom (as Scripture calls it) which now rears and decorates the Temple, now manifests itself in proverb or in parable. The old saws of nations, the majestic precepts of philosophy, the luminous maxims of law, the oracles of individual wisdom, the traditionary rules of truth and justice and religion, even though imbedded in the corruption, or alloyed with the pride, of the world, bespeak His original agency, and His long suffering presence. Even where there is habitual rebellion against Him, or profound, far-spreading social depravity, still the undercurrent, or the heroic outburst of natural virtue, as well as the yearning of the heart after what it has not, and its presentiment of its remedies, are to be ascribed to the Author of all good. Anticipations or reminiscences of His glory haunt the mind of the self-sufficient sage and of the pagan devotee; His writing is upon the wall, whether of the Indian fane or of the porticoes of Greece. He introduces Himself, He all but concurs, according to His good pleasure, and in His selected season, in the issues of unbelief, superstition, and false worship, and changes the character of acts by His overruling operation. He condescends, though He gives no sanction, to the altars and shrines of imposture, and He makes His own fiat the substitute for its sorceries. He speaks amid the incantations of Balaam, raises Samuel's spirit in the witch's cavern, prophesies of the Messias by the tongue of the sybil, forces python to recognise His ministers, and baptises by the hand of the misbeliever. He is with the heathen dramatist in his denunciations of injustice and tyranny, and his auguries of Divine vengeance upon crime. Even on the unseemly legends of a popular mythology He casts His shadow, and is dimly discerned in the ode or the epic, as in troubled water or in fantastic dreams. All that is good, all that is true, all that is beautiful, all that is beneficent, be it great or small, be it perfect or fragmentary, natural as well as supernatural, moral as well as material, comes from Him" ("Discourses on the Scope and Nature of University Education," pp. 91-97).

From all the foregoing considerations, minds tolerably free from prejudice can hardly fail to deduce certain practical conclusions.

1. Worshippers of God are often reproached with seeking to influence their Deity to unduly favour them by the use of flattery; while yet (it is urged) no mere man, if good, would allow himself to be influenced by praises or abject entreaties, or by expressions of reverence and self-abasement, whether by word or gesture. But any one who has gone through the modern controversy as to "the

Unknowable" must logically admit that this reproach and this argument are nothing less than absurd. He must recognise that there is no parity whatever between praise, entreaty, and reverence as addressed to man, and praise, entreaty, and reverence as addressed to God. It is contemptible to flatter men, because it is wrong, and contemptible to say that which we know not to be true; but to flatter God is simply *impossible*. Reverence of an extreme kind paid to man is contemptible, because it is a mode of lying, of asserting a disparity and a superiority which in truth do not exist; but with God it is quite otherwise. No Oriental prostrations can even approximately express the reverence with which *reason* declares it fitting for a creature to approach his Creator, regard being had to that Creator's majesty alone. A worship which by every outward expression should denote a reverence and adoration such as no words could declare would, from this point of view, surely be that which could alone deserve the epithet of *rational*.

2. The recognition of God's inconceivable greatness, joined with our clear perception of all that is implied in our own free will, must force on the student of this modern controversy a special apprehension of the nature of opposition to Him. If "the Unknowable" be all that we are told It is,—if, in other words, God exists, a Being of absolute beauty and holiness, it follows as a

necessary consequence that no other evil can be so great as to be even for a moment comparable with that of a deliberate or habitual denial of worship, or any other act of rebellion against Him. Another consequence also becomes plain; namely, the culpability of those who are careless and indifferent, not caring to inquire seriously and deeply into the truths of religion. Nay, a state of mind which enters upon such an inquiry with the same placidity that befits an inquiry into some purely historical or critical problem is also blameworthy. It is blameworthy, because a will rightly directed cannot but lead its possessor to most earnestly desire that the doctrines of natural religion (the existence of an all holy God, the rewarder in another world of those who strive to follow the dictates of conscience here) may prove to be true. The absence of such desire, then, is in itself a sufficient proof of a bad will. The Author of nature declares to us, through our reason, what, as the Author of grace, He declares through revelation, that "He that is not with Me, is against Me; and he that gathereth not with Me, scattereth."

It thus appears that the true line to be drawn as regards men is between those who have and those who have not a will to adore, love, and serve God. This is taught by the Church in allowing the possibility of salvation to all who, being through no fault of theirs ignorant of revelation, simply worship a *Deus unus et remunerator*, and in affirming that one pure mental act of love of God alone, or with contrition if needed, suffices for justification. Tender consideration and loving sympathy are due to all who reject revealed religion because they cannot see how it accords with their notions of God's perfections. But, unhappily, it is impossible to doubt but that there are men who reject all divine worship because they will submit to no being whatever, and who even pass on to "hate God" with all their heart, with all their soul, with all their mind, and with all their strength; thus beginning, even in this world, a hatred of their Creator which may exist eternally.

3. These considerations, as the present writer has elsewhere * observed, cannot but bring home to the student how evidently true is the saying that God's ways cannot be as our ways, and how, therefore, "the action which we discover immanent in the material universe may be rationally taken to be from God. In that universe we find an action the results of which harmonise with man's reason, which is orderly, which disaccords with the action of blind chance and with the 'fortuitous concourse of atoms' of Democritus; but, at the same time, an action which ever, in part and in ultimate analysis, eludes our grasp, and the modes of which are different from those by which we should have attempted to accomplish such

---

* "Lessons from Nature," p. 374.

ends. The inconsistency is surely very great of those who assert that all our knowledge comes from experience, and at the same time that 'creative action' is incredible, because nature affords no evidence of it. It is so great, because that action must necessarily be unperceived and uncomprehended by us, since of creative action we have and can have no experience whatever. The action of God must necessarily be unimaginable by us in its fulness, but its reality and efficiency can be very clearly conceived as incessant and universal in every form of being known to us. God is thus neither withdrawn from nor identified with His material creation, and no part of it is left devoid of meaning or of purpose. The poet's plaint as to the flower 'born to blush unseen and waste its sweetness on the desert air' is thus manifestly uncalled for—every creature of every order of existence being ever, while its existence is sustained, so complacently contemplated by God, that the intense and concentrated attention of all men of science together upon it could but form an utterly inadequate symbol of such divine contemplation."

4. There is yet one more practical consideration which this controversy seems well fitted to bring home vividly to the student of it; namely, the question of "worship." The consistent evolutionist, who fully apprehends the great principle of continuity, must recognise the utter hopelessness of any one inventing *de novo* a form of worship of "the Unknowable" capable of satisfying the

intellectual, moral, and æsthetic tendencies of men of culture. Perceiving the fact that the ascending process of evolution is "integrating" and not "disintegrating," and that, speaking broadly and on the whole, the later developments are superior to the earlier, it seems inevitable that the rational and consistent evolutionist should go to mass.

Recognising "the Unknowable" as everywhere present in nature, the evolutionist must recognise that a fitting worship shall embrace as wide a field of existences and activities as is compatible with historical evolution. He will not affect to despise the senses and emotions any more than the intellect as involved in such worship; rather, being impressed (as a follower of Herbert Spencer) with the vivid permeability of those channels which lead to irreligious emotions, he will see the reasonableness of facilitating religious emotion by supplying it with easily permeable channels, and of bringing in as much as possible instead of excluding vivid sensations.

In the various fragmentary relics of the Church's worship which have been adopted by the sects, the reason of the evolutionist can hardly fail to be tried and irritated by a service (which is a product of mere disintegrating action) in which worship consists of sentences distinctly uttered in the vernacular tongue, followed by a sermon with which it is very likely he will have but little sympathy. At mass his intellect, though amply exercised, should he so will it, yet need not be tried by the hearing of a single word from beginning to end. His æsthetical instincts may be gratified by treasures of the organic and inorganic worlds, by products of human skill, whether of the artisan or the musician, and by the solemn movements and stately rhythms of motion incident to the sacred rite. His historical sentiments will be gratified by contemplating a worship essentially the same as that spread over our land before these last three centuries of repression; a worship the same as that which aided to weld together Normans and Saxons into our English race; the same as that which has afforded spiritual support to all those the world has deemed most holy—to Fénelon, Vincent of Paul, Aquinas, Francis, and Augustine. Even dimly, as in a glimmering twilight, he may see in the sacred offerings and the accompaniments of flowers, of tapers, and of perfumes, suggestions of a past, remote indeed, even of the early worship of his primitive Aryan forefathers in their Eastern home. The "reasonable service" of Him who is at once the source and maintainer of all evolution from the merely physical to that of human society should surely have this harmonious universality of character. If "the Unknowable," if Almighty God is to be worshipped at all, the consistent evolutionist must surely deem that worship to be most fitting which has thus from century to century grown on and on in one progressive process of increasing integration. The evolutionist, recognising the First Cause everywhere, and also (if a consistent follower of Mr. Spencer) recognising the need of religion, must require a real worship of profound, at least mentally prostrate, adoration of that Cause as actually present here and now. Such a one could not surely find a more fitting mode of worship than the one suggested. Being himself a creature under conditions of space and time, and necessitated to frame his thoughts according to such conditions, he must worship, if he worship at all, the First Cause under those limitations. In joining in worship at the elevation of the host he cannot err, since, as he admits his Deity everywhere, he must surely be also THERE. Nay, he must needs admit that He is emphatically and supereminently there in that which is the centre of devotion to those present, and which has been the centre of devotion and worship of all the holiest souls the world has seen for many centuries past.

But if the follower of Herbert Spencer, convinced of the existence of an inconceivably high First Cause, which, from reverence alone, he refrains from calling personal, should so assist at the Church's highest act of worship, *every doubter as to theism* may rationally also so assist. In offering a hypothetical worship such doubter palters with no truth, but only manifests his goodwill to perform a duty, should the existence of such duty be a reality, as to which, by the hypothesis, he is in a state of uncertainty. If he is sincerely desirous of having his doubts resolved, surely he must feel convinced that such a manifestation of goodwill can have no other than a beneficial effect (supposing a personal First Cause exists) while in no case can it harm or degrade him, since he is not supposed to give any assent to that which he does not really accept, but being confessedly in a state of doubt, he offers only a hypothetical worship, such as should rationally accompany the existence of such doubt, though not, of course, the existence of a state of positive and absolute negation, such as hardly any modern English philosopher openly avows.

Glancing backwards over the course we have traversed, it seems borne in upon us that the logical development of that process which Philip the Fair began is probably advancing, however slowly, to a result very generally unforeseen. But if such result as that here indicated be the probable outcome of philosophical evolution, Christianity has once more evidently nothing whatever to fear from it. A philosophy which as a complement unites in one all other systems, will harmonise with a Religion which as a complement synthesises all other religions, and not only religions properly so-called, but atheism also.

Atheism, pantheism, and pure deism running their

logical course, and mutually refuting each other, find an ultimate synthesis in Christianity, as we have before found them to do in nature. Christianity affirms the truth latent in atheism, namely, that God, as He is, is unimaginable and inscrutable by us; in other words, no such God as we can *imagine* exists. It also affirms the truth in pantheism, that God acts in every action of every created thing, and that in Him we live and move and are. Finally, it also asserts the truth of deism, but by its other assertions escapes the objections to which deism by itself is liable from opposing systems. Similarly, Christianity also effects a synthesis between theism and the worship of humanity, and that by the path not of destruction, but through the nobler conception of "taking the manhood into God."

It may be well to conclude this chapter by a retrospect.

Our investigations concerning social, political, scientific, and philosophic evolution have but led us to what we might have *à priori* anticipated—the conclusion that the highest and most intellectual power is that which must ultimately dominate the inferior forces. Neither political nor scientific developments can avail against the necessary consequences of philosophical evolution. No mistake can be greater than that of supposing that philosophy is but a mental luxury for the few. An implicit, unconscious philosophy possesses the mind and influences the conduct of every peasant. Metaphysical doctrines, sooner or later, filter down from the cultured few to the lowest social strata, and become, for good or ill, the very marrow of the bones, first of a school, then of a society, ultimately of a nation. The course of general philosophy, it is here contended, is now returning to its legitimate channel after a divergence of some three centuries' duration. This return cannot affect prejudicially the Christian Church, but must strengthen and aid it, and thus that beneficial action upon it of political and scientific evolution, before represented as probable, will be greatly intensified, and the great movement of the RENAISSANCE hereafter take its place as the manifestly efficient promoter of a new development of the Christian organism such as the first twenty centuries of its life afforded it no opportunity to manifest.

CHAPTER VI.

ÆSTHETIC EVOLUTION.

IF the reasoning hereinbefore put forward is correct, the influences of social, political, scientific, and philosophical evolution can have no other ultimate effect than that of strengthening and advancing the Christian Church. It might then be expected by the reader that a further question should next be considered, namely, one concerning that evolution of religion itself which is now taking place around us—its antecedents, its present action, its results; and this would form a most deeply interesting subject of inquiry. For the Christian religion claims to be not the true religion, but simply religion—the only religion which ever was, is, or shall be. The patent fact that various forms of heathenism have existed, exist, and will for a time continue to exist, is not of course denied; but it is asserted that all these religions differ from the Christian as being fragmentary, distorted, and therefore misleading representations of the one great truth conveyed to us in its entirety by Christianity, just as the Church itself differs from the sects as being the synthesis of all those truths they severally hold. The religion of the Christian Church claims to differ from all other systems, heathen or Christian, not as one coloured ray of light differs from another—the violet from the red of the solar spectrum,—but as white light differs from all the coloured lights as being the synthesis resulting from their harmonious blending in one perfect unity.

Now were we to treat of the process of religious evolution which we see going on about us, that process might be regarded as it takes place within and without the great Christian organism. But the evolutionary process within the Church has been once for all elucidated with a master hand by Dr. Newman in his great work on "The Development of Christian Doctrine;" and it is well worthy of remark, that this contribution to the great theory of evolution was one of the first. Its sagacious author anticipated the doctrines of Spencer, of Darwin, and of Haeckel, though he restrained their application strictly within the area of his proper subject. It should not be forgotten by those who esteem so highly the doctrine of evolution, that almost the first, and perhaps the most solid and enduring contribution towards it, was in the domain of theology, and by one of the most uncompromising supporters of sacerdotalism and the supernatural.

It would be presumptuous for one who is no theologian to attempt to follow in such footsteps. It will be enough to observe that the generation which has gone by since that era-marking work appeared has apparently justified its assertions and predictions. The culmination of the process has been the great Vatican decree, the keystone of the great arch of civil and religious liberty,—a decree which Germany now proves to us to have been dictated by a more than mortal prescience.

As to the characters presented by contemporary religious evolution outside the Church, we have already, in the first chapter, pointed out that the religious disruption of the sixteenth century resulted in two distinct yet intermixed processes and tendencies. One of these was simply distinctive and pagan, and has ended in the widespread negation of all religion which we see in Germany to-day. The other was the formation of the various sects, such as Lutheranism, Calvinism, Anglicanism, Puritanism, etc., etc. In the present day it is sufficiently obvious that these various religious bodies are undergoing a more or less slow process of disruption and dissolution, and their adherents tending, with greater or less rapidity, either towards anti-theism on the one hand or towards the Church upon the other.

Closely connected, however, with the evolution of religion is that of æsthetic evolution; and this essay may perhaps be fitly closed by an endeavour to pourtray some few of the probable effects of the great modern movement of contemporary evolution upon Christian art.

It is generally admitted that art has been profoundly affected by Christianity. The effect was indeed gradual, and the changes which have taken place from the second and third century have been due to the action of many other causes also, but it cannot be contested but that Christianity has been at least one of the most important of them. Christian art as regards architecture culminated in the thirteenth century. Sculpture and painting continued to develop at the least until the end of the sixteenth century; but as they gained in natural beauty they lost the Christian inspiration, and the nature of the artistic movement of the Renaissance has been already noted in the first chapter.*

Now the greatest lover of Christian art, if he is candid cannot deny the various imperfections of its early and mediæval efforts, nor the great improvement and advance which in many respects marked the reappearance of the pagan spirit in art.

Are we then to anticipate a complete severance between high art and Christian symbolism of all kinds; or may we hope that the decay of Christian art has been but the prelude to its reappearance in a more perfect condition hereafter, as the break up of the harmony of the grub or *larva* into the discord of the chrysalis or *pupa*, results in the more perfect harmony of the *imago*, or butterfly?

In the present day we have seen a great reaction against the Renaissance movement,—architecturally in modern gothic, pictorially in the school of Overbeck and pre-Raphaelism, and musically in a return to Palestrina and

---

* See *ante*, page 24.

Gregorian Church singing. In sculpture, the reversion has been less marked, yet it may be traced in many monumental effigies.

Still, nothing we have yet seen is, it must be confessed, very encouraging. In order that this artistic evolution should follow the general law, it should present us with examples of a progress from a comparatively undifferentiated and simple beginning to a complex and heterogeneous result.

Now as regards MUSIC, the very controversies which take place about it show that we have arrived at a new conception ; namely, the appropriateness of different styles for different purposes. When the Gregorian style was young, it was the general style of the day, and had no special sacredness.

Similarly, the styles which succeeded were forms of the fashion of their period, and the praises of love or wine were celebrated in the same manner as the praise of Christ and His saints. We have, then, now a new idea to work upon, with immensely enriched materials, and music is becoming curiously and deliberately Christian in a way it never was before. Gregorian singing and the music of Palestrina are made use of with a distinctly Christian feeling and intention ; and however different may be the musical expression of the Christian religious sentiment in the time to come, the foundations of its distinctness are already laid, and its differentiation is determined.

In PAINTING, the beauty as to devotional expression and religious conception of Fra Angelico and painters of kindred schools was of course marred by a defective knowledge of anatomy and many technical defects. Yet how superior are such works in religious expression to later works, in other respects so superior! The process of evolution in this art has now already given us two distinct styles—sources of endless enjoyment—the landscape and the historical picture. The third style, the religious, is yet in embryo; but we have already its conception—the idea of painting consciously Christian, and separate from other styles to a degree never thought of before, yet making use of all the improvements which the last three centuries have introduced.

Nevertheless, purely realistic painting and naturalism, most suitable for landscape and historical subjects, are now recognised as inappropriate, save as regards subordinate details, in attempts to pourtray what is infinitely beyond human imagination. Purely religious subjects, it is recognised, can only be pourtrayed symbolically; and in order so to pourtray them, more may be learnt from the devotional treatment and expression of earlier days than from the artistic triumphs of later centuries.

Precisely the same considerations apply to SCULPTURE. A development of this art may well, however, take place in connection with religion beyond anything seen in former days. It may do so, because when the absurdity of trying to do away with sacred images and image worship is fully realised, the use of such may be expected greatly to increase. The absurdity of trying to do without images will be appreciated at its just value when the spread of philosophy will have made it axiomatic that we cannot even think but by the help of sensible images in our minds. The most rigid Puritan, the strictest Mahometan, cannot worship without worshipping images—the images of his own imagination formed by his own brain—images in our own day far from likely to be taken for realities (taken as objectively agreeing with what they represent), and therefore far more misleading than any solid images of wood or stone, against the adequacy of which, as representatives of the divine, we are fully on our guard.

In ARCHITECTURE again we have now developed a distinction which certainly did not exist in mediæval times—that between sacred and secular buildings. Then all buildings were essentially of one style, and the refectory, or hall of justice, if of sufficient dimensions, might hardly be distinguishable from the nave of a church. The form, however, which church architecture should assume is a matter of keen debate, and mostly between the advocates of the pointed style and those who admire modern Italian architecture for church purposes. The arguments by which these two views are supported have been put forward in two articles which appeared in the *Dublin Re-*

view, and a consideration of them, as types of two schools, may serve to bring forward the author's views as to the probable effect of the progress of modern evolution on Christian church architecture.

The first of these articles was by an author who signed himself H. W. B., and it appeared in the April number of the *Dublin Review* for 1872. The second article appeared in the January number of the succeeding year. The first article advocated the employment of the "gothic" style in our church architecture. The second article gave the preference very decidedly to the "Italian."

H. W. B. advances the following arguments in favour of the employment of "gothic" in our churches :—(1) It was re-introduced amongst Catholics by the great and good Bishop Milner; (2) it is the only architecture which has originated under Christian influences; (3) it is the style at present popular for ecclesiastical buildings; (4) it is capable of adaptation to all needs; (5) its use is now widely diffused over both hemispheres; (6) it is cheap. The writer further controverts the allegations of such anti-goths as maintain :—(1) That gothic is anti-Roman; (2) that it causes the obstruction of church interiors by too many columns; (3) that gothic churches are dark; (4) that they are cold ; (5) that their constructive peculiarities cause the altar to be hidden from a large part of the congregation. In opposition to these five assertions, H. W. B. contends :—(1) That, far from being anti-Roman, gothic is adopted by the zealous and uncompromising ultramontanes of Germany and Holland; (2) that many columns and narrow naves are by no means necessary features of gothic (instancing the cathedrals of Alby and Angers, seventy feet wide, that of Angoulême without columns, and that of Terragona, in Spain, eighty feet wide); (3) that gothic is the style which is *par excellence* capable of admitting light, some of its structures being almost all window, while Italian churches, like St. Paul's, alone of English cathedrals, is incapable of being photographed internally; (4) that gothic churches can just as easily be made warm as Italian ones; and (5) that the altar can as easily be made visible to the congregation in gothic as in any other style of architecture. This writer, on the other hand, fully admits that a real and complete Italian church is a fine and noble thing, but contends that those generally built (or likely to be built by us in England now) resemble mere unsightly rooms. Expense alone, he asserts, would prevent the erection of really fine Italian churches in England, an elaborate stucco ceiling (like that of S. Peter in Montorio, in Rome) being likely to cost more than would a stone vault, even if that stone were marble.

The other writer, the advocate of "Italian" church architecture, opposes H. W. B., and replies to the follow-

* *Dublin Review*, January, 1873, Art. v., p. 105.

ing effect. He begins by conceding * that there is no force in those five objections to gothic just noticed as anti-Roman, over-columned, dark, cold, or hiding the altar. These concessions are, however, followed by the following hostile assertions:—He says (1) that gothic churches are ill adapted to the existing exigencies of Catholic worship; (2) that they are unsuited to the use of paintings; (3) that they are also unfavourable to the use of sacred images, which latter were, he asserts, in gothic architecture too much subordinated to architectural features; his chief contention, however, is (4) that a majestic "unity" finds expression in almost every Italian church, while in gothic ones unity is lost in multiplicity of detail and complexity of design. He asserts again and again that a church should be the material expression of a divine religious unity which can be apprehended "at one glance,"—that it should be well adapted to the most recent developments of ritual, and especially harmonious with the modern religious developments of the pictorial and plastic arts. He also maintains that an Italian church need not cost more than a similarly sized gothic one; and to the affirmation that a common structure of the former style is a mere "room," he rejoins by stigmatising an inferior gothic one as a mere "barn."

Now it is not probable that the first of these writers would deny the needfulness of the positive characters for which the second writer contends, nor that the second would repudiate the advantages desiderated by the first. We may therefore venture to *combine* their requirements as to the style of architecture really suited for a Christian church. They will be as follows:—(1) That it should be connected with saintly memories of the past; (2) that it should have originated and have been greatly modified through Christian influences; (3) that it should be widely acceptable; (4) that it should be capable of adaptation to varied circumstances; (5) that it should not be anti-Roman; (6) that it should be exactly fitted to our existing modes of worship; (7) that it should not necessitate too many columns; (8) that it should not exclude a due amount of light; (9) that it should not render heating exceptionally difficult; (10) that it should manifest one predominant idea and exhibit an impressive unity; (11) that it should afford good spaces for the effective exhibition of paintings; (12) that it should harmonise with the use of sacred images according to existing modes; (13) that it should not be extraordinarily expensive. To these requirements I would venture to add: (14) that it should be eminently rational as well as beautiful, so as to be a fitting shrine for our "reasonable service."

By the word "gothic" is here meant the successive styles of architecture which prevailed from the very earliest "early English"—or its Continental equivalent

—down to the latest "perpendicular" or "flamboyant." But these styles are in many respects so diverse, that it is difficult to find for them any common character other than that of the employment of the pointed arch, which runs through them all in the smallest ornamental details as well as in the main constructive features, and profoundly modifies and dominates the whole. Thus the phrase "the pointed style," so commonly adopted to denote what many call "gothic," is one admirably chosen for its purpose, the pointed arch being the one governing character of all forms of gothic. The word "Italian," as here used, denotes that style which has prevailed generally, but especially in Italy, from the full development of the transitional Renaissance down to the revival of pointed architecture. As notable examples may be taken S. Peter's, S. Andrea della Valle, and the Gesu, of Rome; S. Paul's, of London; the Pantheon and S. Sulpice, of Paris. For the church architecture of this post-mediæval period it is perhaps more difficult to find any positive common character than for gothic architecture. Perhaps it may best be shortly described as "round-arched," with ornamental details copied exclusively from or directly suggested by pre-Christian Roman and Greek authorities, with a tendency to the use of the dome.

The lovers or advocates of the pointed style may well contend that as to the first two of the fourteen requirements above enumerated it is unrivalled. Centuries must indeed elapse before any later style can boast as many *saintly associations* as can that one which ranged from the birth of S. Bernard to that of S. Ignatius. These associations, moreover, have especial force in England, owing to the apostasy which synchronised with the abandonment of that style. Again, it is evident that no other style is so emphatically and exclusively *Christian in its origin.*

It may also be fairly maintained that gothic is now *widely acceptable;* but it should not be forgotten there is also a wide-spread hostility to its use, and that with the very congregation with which the recent spread of the Church in England is so signally connected—the Oratorian, it does not appear to have found favour. Far be it from me to be faint in acknowledging the deference due to the judgment of our immortal Bishop Milner, but there is another authority equally great on the opposite side—that of Dr. Newman. The fourth character, *adaptability to varied circumstances*, is one in which gothic has indeed the advantage over Italian. The very essence of gothic is the subordination of means to ends; irregularity and asymmetry, instead of being blemishes, add to the very attractiveness and picturesqueness of the pointed structures which display them. Not so with Italian architecture—rigid as to its requirements in these respects, all buildings erected in that style must subordinate all details of arrangement to the general design adopted. The next requirement is one of extreme importance and of deep significance—that, namely, of essential *harmony with Rome*.

The arguments brought forward by the first writer are forcible enough. It is most true that thorough-going ultramontanes in France, Germany, and Holland have built in the pointed style, and it may be added even the Society of Jesus itself has habitually, as we all well know, made use of it in England and elsewhere. Nevertheless, there is a mode of favouring gothic which is not only anti-Roman but essentially anti-Christian, and a danger attends the too eager advocacy of the former which in no way attends the most zealous support of Italian architecture.

A strong assertion of the claim of gothic to be *the* "Christian" style, to the exclusion of all others, is almost tantamount to a reproach on the Church for having consented to its abandonment in favour of a revived "pagan" style. It harmonises with the view (so strongly put forward by Michelet in this connection) that Christianity culminated at the period of Innocent III. and S. Louis—at the time of the purest and most perfect gothic architecture, that of the S. Chapelle—and that since then Christianity itself has been progressively decaying and disintegrating.

But the Christian Church, as has been before said,

went forth from the "upper chamber" of Jerusalem conquering and to conquer, and though always "militant" and never yet "triumphant," her course, in spite of apparent superficial reverses, has been in fact a progress from victory to victory. Far from failing in the sixteenth and seventeenth centuries, her Catholicity became even more manifest, more explicitly developed, and more consciously maintained on the part of her spiritual children.

Any position, then, which leads us to view with want of sympathy the *post*-mediæval path of the Church is essentially uncatholic in its tendency, and such a view seems latent in that exclusive and passionate advocacy of the pointed style which has occasionally found expression. It seems to indicate the presence of a preference for the Church as she was at an earlier period, instead of a loyal and undeviating fidelity to the Spouse of Christ, as she exhibits herself to us at this day; and it is where the gothic spirit is strongest out of England, namely, in Germany and Holland, that the heresy of Reinkens has found both its birthplace and anointing.

It is not, of course, contended that gothic is essentially anti-Roman; but it is contended that it is *accidentally* so, as will again appear in connection with the next requirement, namely, *fitness for the existing ritual*. Nothing could have been more admirably adapted for the worship to be carried on within them than were the gothic churches at the time of their erection. Now, however, the assistance of the laity at "office" has all but ceased ; nor have we, nor are we likely to have, troops of canons, regular and secular, to fill the deep stalled chancels and vast enclosed choirs of our mediæval edifices. Almost daily benedictions, frequent expositions, and prayers recited at the altar's foot, to be heard and responded to by the people find in general a more suitable and congruous home in an Italian church than in a *real* gothic structure, which is thus again, to a certain extent, unavoidably anti-Roman. As to the requirement that the interior should not be greatly *obstructed by columns*, it has been demonstrated by the first writer, and admitted by his opponent, that "gothic" by no means necessitates its infringement.

The eighth requirement, that of an adequate supply of light, can equally be met by either style. But the mode of meeting it is different in both, and seems to the present writer to be objectionable in both. As H. W. B. most justly observes, a gothic church may be "all window," as is the case with the noble pointed choir added to the old Dom of Aachen ; and indeed, the pointed style in its fullest development, such as the choir of Beauvais, with large lower windows and with double, glazed triforia as well as clerestory, becomes one enormous lantern. Moreover, these pointed windows, with their graceful tracery, are beautiful objects in themselves, apart from the glorious colours which should fill them. Nevertheless it cannot but be unreasonable and contradictory to provide immense windows for the admission of light and then exclude that very light by the treatment of the material with which such windows are glazed; this appears to be a serious objection, in addition to others which will shortly be noticed in relation to painted windows. Italian architecture is free from this glaring irrationality, but then it is at the expense of presenting ugly and staring gaps for the admission of light, instead of the graceful fenestration of gothic architecture. This objectionable Italian feature is also likely to be much more offensive and obtrusive in our dull climate than it is in Italy, where the exclusion of sunlight is a boon to be desired.

In connection with "light" naturally comes "heat"; but it is difficult to see how any one style can necessarily have any advantage over another with regard to affording facilities for the admission of manufactured warmth.

The tenth requirement proposed was that a church "should manifest one predominant idea and exhibit an impressive unity." I think it must be conceded that the advocate of the Italian style is right when he says, that on entering an Italian church (say S. Peter's or the Gesu), as opposed to a gothic one (say the Cathedral of Canterbury or the Abbey Church of Westminster), one *does* receive an impression of majestic unity rather than of awe-inspiring complexity—that all is, as he says, "taken in at a glance," instead of offering for investigation a series of successive revelations of beauty and mystery. But to very many the absence of this element is one fatal defect in churches of the "Italian" style. How many varied combinations, each as full of interest as of beauty, are presented to us by a magnificent old gothic church, the original complexity of which has been increased by the irregular additions of succeeding centuries! At the same time, though it would be a grievous loss to give up this rich element of surprise and mystery, we need not shrink from admitting that gothic does leave something to be desired as to unity, and does often, as in Canterbury, more or less impoverish the general effect of a building as a whole by excess of subdivision. Most persons would surely admit that a combination would be desirable in which, while a majestic unity should be the prevailing characteristic, a subordinate complexity, presenting unexpected mysterious features and varied combinations, should by no means be excluded.

The next desirable feature of a modern church is that perhaps in which gothic appears at the greatest disadvantage compared with Italian; namely, in the space it affords for the effective exhibition of paintings. In addition to the relatively small unbroken wall (between the many windows and architectural irregularities of surface), the effect of paintings must ever be ruined by the brilliant hues of the material with which every window of a perfect gothic church should be glazed. Thus, in spite of the beauty of stained glass, it has in addition to its intrinsic irrationality the grievous disadvantage of marring, or rather destroying, the effect of perhaps the most important of the arts which minister to religion.*

But not painting alone; sculpture also (as now used for purposes of devotion) finds a place more readily and harmoniously in an Italian than in a gothic church. In the former, holy images can attain both a larger and more independent development than the latter, where each, closely buried in its niche, assumes a quasi-architectural character. The second writer referred to goes on indeed to add that in the gothic style "the images of our Lord and the saints are not representations of our Lord who came in the flesh, or of the saints, who were men of like passions with ourselves. They are as if 'clothed in white samite, mystic, wonderful.'" But this objection seems a very unreasonable one. To assert that mediæval sculpture was necessarily defective, from the imperfect anatomical knowledge of the period, would be reasonable enough; but to object to images which are to suggest to us divine and sanctified beings as they now are *in glory*, because they are "mystic" and "wonderful,"

---

* The church of S. Apollinaris at Remagen is a good example of the incongruity of gothic with paintings.

seems to me a mistake. Surely such are the very characters which such images should present!

Passing by the requirement as to expense, which appears to be about equally capable of fulfilment by either gothic or Italian, we may pass to the last requirement, that, namely, as to the reasonableness which should pervade it and should manifest itself in the constructions it inspires. In this matter it must be allowed that gothic has a most decisive advantage over Italian. Mediæval architecture has developed with admirable skill the art of forming the largest and most durable constructions with the least expenditure of material. It may be called emphatically the most rationalistic and truthful system of stone construction which the world has yet witnessed. That canon for which Mr. Ruskin has had so much credit, but which was, years before, enunciated by Augustus Welby Pugin, "that nothing should be constructed for ornament, but that all construction should be useful first, and secondarily made the vehicle for ornament," is thoroughly embodied in "pointed" architecture alone.

No doubt this rule was occasionally transgressed by mediæval architects, as, *e.g.*, by the designer of the west front of Wells cathedral; but in Italian architecture it is persistently ignored. Thus the erection of flying buttresses is almost a necessity where a massive stone roof is suspended at a great altitude over a spacious interior; but while such buttresses become, in the pointed style, objects of beauty no less than of utility, in the architecture of Italy they have no avowed place, and may be, as in S. Paul's cathedral, concealed by an elaborate screen of stone, which is *doubly* mendacious, since it denies the existence of constructions which it exists only to hide, and at the same time tends to delude the observer as to the real height of the walls, the altitude of which it falsifies by exaggeration. In gothic architecture, wherever a door or a window is really wanted, there it is placed. It is not denied or disguised, but made manifest, and at the same time ornamental.

It would be easy to adduce a multitude of examples, but these are sufficient to illustrate the principle which is here maintained ; namely, that a temple of the God who has given us our reason no less than our æsthetic instincts, and who is truth itself, should be both eminently " rational " and thoroughly " true."

Recapitulating, then, our short examination of the fitness for church architecture of the two styles, gothic and Italian, it seems that neither one nor the other can be deemed free from very serious objections.

But is there no alternative ? Are we externally to oscillate from gothic to Italian, and from Italian to gothic ? Has the Church come to the end of her architectural powers of expression after passing from the catacombs through the basilica to the pointed minster, and back to the classical revival of Italy? Believing, as has been asserted in this essay, that the Church's splendour in the thirteenth century was but a faint adumbration of the august future reserved for her even in this world, and while still only the Church militant, it is probable that architecturally, no less than in other respects, what is yet to be will be far more glorious than anything which yet has been.

Readers may well ask whether there are any grounds for this prediction,—whether the invention of a new style is to be expected. Certainly no style was ever formed, nor, is it probable that one will ever be formed, otherwise than by gradual growth. Yet there *does* seem to be evidence of the possibility of such future growth. A zealous Italian may say, "You have objected to extreme gothicism as opposing a Church of the past to the Church of to-day, and as blaming its action in the post-mediæval period; but you yourself implicitly blame that period when you abuse the mendacity and other failings of the architecture which during that period it formed. This criticism would, however, be very erroneous. We do *not* blame the course pursued in adopting and developing the Renaissance; on the contrary, we believe it to have been the only wise and proper action then possible. But it is one thing to say that an action was, under given circumstances, the relatively best, and quite another to say that such action would be, under all circumstances, the absolutely best.

If what is here advocated should find favour, it would none the less have been impossible at the period referred to. The Renaissance and subsequent architecture was a necessary transitional step; the return to pagan models was, probably, the only mode possible for progress, even if that progress should hereafter take the course here suggested. "*Reculer pour mieux sauter*" will then be found to have been the real signification of the retrogression, although, of course, the actual enthusiasts for classical revivals were not conscious of the future which they were, in fact, but beginning to prepare.

We would urge then, that while full of veneration for every manifestation of the Church, while reverencing its outward expression from the first to the nineteenth centuries, we should carefully keep ourselves clear from all *exclusive* attachment to any one of those passing modes —whether basilican, gothic, Italian, or what not—in which its spirit found material expression, In the words of the first writer here referred to,* we should be careful not "to adore the works themselves instead of the God who inspired them," or "to worship the mere garments in which the Church has decked herself." The view taken by fanatical admirers of "Christian" (*i. e.*, pointed) architecture is very different from that taken by the mediæval builders themselves, who actually fancied that *they* were

---

* *Loc. cit.*, p. 449.

continuing true classical architecture, just as the German kaisers were, in their eyes, real successors of Cæsar and the Antonines.

It is time now to explain exactly where the development is to be looked for of a new style of architecture combining the advantages and avoiding the defects of both the Italian and the gothic styles. As was said at starting, the pointed arch is the one dominant feature of gothic architecture, and it is so with good reason, if, as we believe, the whole mode of architectural development in the thirteenth, fourteenth, and fifteenth centuries was due to the introduction of the pointed arch in the twelfth. That element, once introduced, gave as it were a certain twist to architecture, which, once having got into the pointed groove, ran its natural course and worked itself thoroughly out. Having reached its last stage, no richness of detail in panelled wall or fantraceried vault could compensate for the weariness produced by endless mechanical repetition, where the same ornamental features were reproduced on all sides, so as to suggest their being carried down to microscopic dimensions. Great indeed must have been the feeling of relief afforded by the change to a revived classicism. We may speculate as to the possibilities of architectural development had no classical Renaissance taken place, and there are facts enough to make us rejoice over that Renaissance, as at least a relative blessing, compared with what might otherwise have been in store for us.

When we consider the wonderful pulpits of Belgium —with their apes and parrots—and certain late churches, where the pillars expand above into realistic reproductions of palm-trees, the possibility suggests itself that, but for the classical revival, our churches might have assumed such a realistic botanical and zoological development as to have become like immense structures of Dresden china transformed into stone, its pillars stone trees, its window-tracery a collection of petrified creepers, its niches grottos, and its altars rocks!

If, however, nothing further is to be hoped from gothic, and if we can nevertheless only hope for something new by a more or less continuous development from something old, what is to be our starting point? As has been said, gothic architecture is essentially pointed, and its *raison d'être* is the pointed arch. To obtain a new starting-point, continuous with preceding structures, we must then revert to architecture as it existed before, or independently of, the introduction of the pointed arch. Now, of such architecture we fortunately have abundant examples in Germany, where the pointed arch appeared late, was for a long time sparingly adopted, the pre-existing round-arched or Romanesque style persisting.

We have in the cathedral of Speyer a magnificent example of this style in its earlier condition, that of excessive strength and stability; but from this early

Romanesque a lighter round-arched style became developed, embodying the true principles of construction and much of the picturesqueness of gothic, while free from the special peculiarity of pointed arches and details. There is much reason to believe that if the pointed arch had not made its appearance in Germany at all, a style would have been ultimately developed at least as perfect as the true gothic subsequently became. But this development was nipped in the bud by the introduction, first of the pointed arch, and then of true *French* gothic, like that of Cologne cathedral.

It is here contended that we must have recourse to the Romanesque, not for adoption and imitation, but as a starting-point whence to develop an architecture at once rational and beautiful, embodying all the truest and best principles of construction and ornamentation, and profiting by and learning from both pointed architecture and from all that was admirable in the Renaissance of Italy. It is not meant that we are to become architectural eclectics, and cull a feature here from the gothic, there from the Renaissance—a window from Lincoln, an arch from Italy, etc. It is meant that the architect should endeavour to improve upon the Romanesque by a mind imbued with all that is best, both in the spirit of true gothic and of the Renaissance. In this way I believe it possible that a style of church-building may be evolved which shall satisfy all the requirements drawn out in the earlier part of this chapter. This we will endeavour shortly to show; but first it may be useful to notice some of the old more or less perfectly Romanesque churches, which may serve, not as models, but as objects of study, full of fruitful suggestions.

Foremost amongst these may perhaps be cited S. Cunibert's at Cologne, which, although finished in the same year in which the cathedral was begun, nevertheless exhibits the pointed arch only here and there. It consists of a nave and aisles with clerestory, an apsidal choir, having on each side a tower. At the west end is a lofty transept, somewhat as in our old college chapels, as *e.g.*, at Magdalen College, Oxford.

Again, the Apostles' Church, with its three apsides, and that of S. Martin's, with its short sanctuary, so suitable for modern worship, as well as the grand old church of Andernach and the Abbey of Maria Laach, should be carefully studied. The lovely fragment still left of the abbey church of Heisterbach may be referred to as an example of the lightness and elegance attained to in the transition period, as the cathedral of Maintz, and that, before referred to, of Speyer, may be quoted as examples of the majestic solidity of the earlier Romanesque.

S. Gereon's church at Cologne shows how fine an effect might be produced by the addition of the dome to Romanesque architecture; while the peculiar semi-circular windows of St. Cunibert's, as also of the nave of the minster at Bonn, suggest the employment of windows at once ornamental and light-giving, yet not absorbing too much space.

The cathedral of Durham and the city of Shrewsbury show us how light and beautiful a development the round arch sometimes attained even in England; but it is in Germany that by far the richest collection will be found of round-arched buildings calculated to suggest treatment and features suitable for modern round-arched buildings constructed on the *principles*, though not in the *configuration*, of mediæval, pointed architecture.*

It is much to be regretted that so many of our architects have been so tied down and cramped by the narrow taste of their public for "middle-pointed" architecture with abundant floral ornamentation. We know more than one who groans over the apparent impossibility of introducing a taste for grand and solid buildings of real majesty, instead of the "pretty" and petty beauties so generally in vogue. Those readers interested in

---

* Many of these German churches have an apse at each end. It appears to me that this feature might be very usefully adopted with a slight modification, the western apse serving as a baptistery. As we are "buried with Christ in baptism," a representation of the entombment might be appropriately placed in a small crypt beneath the font in such western baptismal apse.

some parish church about to be built may profitably make a pilgrimage to S. Columba's, Shoreditch, and imagine the excellent effect of similar buildings, the designer being invited to discard in them the pointed arch except where solidity or convenience of construction might require it.

Let us now review the style of church architecture here suggested as regards the fourteen requirements enumerated in the earlier part of this communication. In the first place, as it adopts its principles of construction and ornamentation mainly from mediæval architecture, it can claim a share in the holy memories connected with the latter, while, in its repudiation of the narrowness of gothic, it is in harmony with the spirit of St. Philip and the saintly men of the post-Tridentine period.

The same considerations show that it fulfils the second requirement, that, namely, of having been "originated through Christian influences." The third requirement, "that it should be widely acceptable," is one which it is already well on the way to fulfil. In France, in Belgium, in Germany, and even in England, symptoms of a spontaneous and apparently unconscious development in this direction are already to be met with.

The next requirement, "that it should be capable of adaptation to all needs," is of the very essence of its *principles*, which are those of mediæval architecture, it not being in the least tied down to the formality and symmetry of the Italian style.

"That it should not be anti-Roman" is also of its essence, since it will arise in part from an objection to gothic as being to a certain degree open to that reproach, and since it will freely adopt all the best features of the Italian style.

"That it should be exactly fitted to our existing modes of worship" will also necessarily follow, since it will be developed with the express purpose of providing in the best manner possible to harmonise with and subserve the ritual of the period of its birth. The seventh requirement, "that there should not be too many columns," also follows, since it is free to adopt in this respect whatever features in whatever preceding style may be deemed most desirable. The eighth requirement, that respecting the due admission of "light," is one in which it will present numerous important advantages over every preceding style.

In the first place, the absence of any rigid rule of symmetry will allow the admission of light just whenever it may be required. Secondly, the windows may be of any shape found the most convenient,—square, elongated, and narrow windows, rose-windows or semi-circular windows, as in the nave of Bonn cathedral. They may also be made ornamental by mullions, while tracery need not by any means be confined to the upper part of each window, since each window may be all tracery, the stonework being of such thickness as may combine strength and security with a copious admission of light. The absence of that beautiful but self-contradictory feature, *brilliant* stained glass, will allow an ample supply of light without too great a sacrifice of wall-space, and without any impairment of stability. Not that the glazing should not be ornamental and artistic; the pieces of glass might be so designed that their lead framework may form elegant patterns,* while the glass itself, of delicate greys and half-tints, will afford a wide scope for the skilful designer. The nature and arrangement of the windows will especially facilitate the eleventh requirement—that as to paintings,—since the neutral-tinted glass will be highly favourable, while the non-obstruction offered by it to the entrance of light will by rendering less numerous or less large windows necessary, increase the amount of available wall-space.

The preceding requirement that each church should "manifest one predominant idea, and exhibit an impressive unity," can as well be met by the developed Romanesque as by Italian architecture. That noble and

---

* A precedent for this is to be found in the abbey of Pontigny. This abbey was built in the early days of the Cistercian reform, and the luxury of stained glass having been forbidden, an ornamental arrangement of colourless glass by means of the leading became the only adornment.

especially unity-giving structure "the dome" will find its place therein; and there is no noble feature of the Italian style that may not be freely adopted in the style I venture to advocate. At the same time, the absence of any rigid canons as to symmetry will allow the free development of all such subordinate features or later added additions in each building as original or subsequent needs may require, and thus an element of complexity, surprise, and mystery may be annexed, in a secondary manner, to the predominant and primary unity of the whole.

It is hardly necessary to add that the modern use of holy images will here meet with facilities fully as great as in Italian architecture, and a different degree of prominence, importance, or majesty, can readily be given to each separate image.

Finally, that requirement as to church architecture which has been here added to those of H. W. B. and his opponent, namely, rationality of construction, will find itself pre-eminently met in the architecture here advocated. It will be so that because the adaptation of all the true principles of mediæval architecture is one of the primary conditions supposed and laid down for its development, while whatever is noble and striking in post-mediæval architecture may be freely adopted; nevertheless, its various objectionable features will be as studiously eschewed.

Thus a concordat may be established between those rival parties the "Goths" and the "Italians," and we shall cease to be "cabined, cribbed, confined" within the narrow limits of the last six centuries.

If we are right in believing that the Church will, even in this world, attain a majesty and glory such as was but poorly shadowed forth by its mediæval beauty, it is surely reasonable also to believe that the artistic expression of its spirit has as yet by no means fully blossomed forth, and an undue exaltation of the post-mediæval art of Italy is surely to be deprecated as strongly as are the exaggerated claims made by some for the style which preceded it.

Should it one day, by God's permission, whether by war, by natural convulsion, or the violence of demagogic passion, be demolished, there is no need to doubt but that afterwards another S. Peter's would arise as much excelling in majesty and beauty the S. Peter's we see to-day as the S. Peter's of to-day excels the ancient and venerable basilica of Constantine which preceded it.

H. W. B.'s opponent himself makes* the following remark: "That different ideas of the human mind are expressed by different styles of architecture will hardly be denied by any who have thought upon the subject. If this be granted, then it is difficult to see how any

---

* Loc. cit., p. 107.

one style of architecture can be upheld to the exclusion of all others." This seems to be in one sense true, and in another sense false. That any one style of architecture is suitable for all times and all places is manifestly absurd; but nevertheless, we may surely maintain that only one style can be really suitable for a definite purpose at any special locality at any given period.

If it is true, as the writer just quoted says, that "different ideas" are expressed by "different styles," we hold it to be also true that one definite and clear idea can have but one distinct and articulate architectural expression. We also believe that every church built should be the expression and embodiment of its religious object as conceived at the period of its erection in the locality in which it is placed.

While this rule is by no means a narrow one, but freely allows that various and diverse buildings (*e.g.*, Amiens, or the Certosa of Pavia, or the Gesu) may correctly embody the diverse ideas of their designers, it is decisive against the fitness of either gothic or Italian for the religious architecture of the future in England. That which correctly embodied conceptions of the thirteenth century, or the Italian climate, *cannot* also be the correct embodiment of an English devotional idea of the nineteenth century, except such idea is of the essential identity of the Church of to-day with that of the Middle Ages. As such an idea of continuity has largely occupied the minds of English Catholics since Catholic emancipation, it has been nationally and fittingly expressed by the architecture we have in the main hitherto adopted. What could be more satisfying to the mind of an English Catholic at the end of three centuries of persecution than to see rising on every side church and chapel, convent and cloister, the very same with those of which their forefathers had been formerly deprived! What a poem can be read in the stones of S. Augustine's, Ramsgate! How complete is the resuscitation presented to us by the Black Friars of Woodchester! For some time to come gothic architecture will still be fitly used, and surely it might be well that the metropolitan church of Westminster should visibly and tangibly declare the spiritual authority ruling in it to be the legitimate successor and representative of the extinct primacy of the abolished province of Canterbury.

That providential action which favoured the classical Renaissance, and which did away with the narrowness of pointed architecture has no less presided over the great mediæval revival which has spread so widely over the earth with such happy results. But in the nature of things such an architectural protest cannot be continual. The continuity and unity of the Church of the nineteenth century with that of the thirteenth having been by the recent happy revival once for all architecturally demonstrated, the devotional idea will surely cease to be occupied therewith, and will address itself to the direct object of the buildings it erects without an eternal retrospect on any particular period. Such ideas will not improbably find their architectural embodiments in some such development as that here advocated. Therein and thereby all wants and aspirations will find their satisfaction ; and while the actions of the Church in this matter in different preceding epochs will all alike be justified, we shall none the less be encouraged to look forward to other developments and greater glories of religious art than any revealed to us in the course of the centuries which are gone. *Nullum tempus occurrit ecclesiæ!* The ever fruitful mother of beauty and of truth, of holy aspirations and of good works, has not come to the end of her evolution even in the world of art, and one mode has been here indicated in which that evolution may be advantageously worked out.

Recurring to what has been said as to the other arts besides architecture, it may, then, in conclusion, be affirmed that there appear to be grounds for thinking that in the whole field of art, music, painting, sculpture, and architecture, our successors may witness a vast, new, complex, and stable artistic integration of a special and distinctly Christian character—a self-consciousness, as it were, in Christian art such as never was before, and which will appropriately serve to externally clothe and embody that vast and magnificent Christian development for which the modern phases of political, scientific, and philosophic evolution are, if the views here put forward are just and true, surely preparing the way at a future period; to which Christians may look forward with joy and hope, but without a shadow of impatience, being abundantly thankful if the providence of God graciously grants them the opportunity of helping forward in their own day, in however insignificant a degree, that great scheme, which, as all theists are rationally compelled to allow, is the one supreme end of the whole evolutionary process, so far as the great Author of nature has revealed His purposes to our eyes, not merely by supernatural revelation, but also by that great natural revelation which the universe, as manifested in mind as well as in matter, displays to the eyes of every one who duly ponders without prejudice over the lessons it conveys.

www.ingramcontent.com/pod-product-compliance
Lightning Source LLC
Chambersburg PA
CBHW031351230426
43670CB00006B/502